Historical Thinking Skills Workbook

A Workbook for European History

John P. Irish

Carroll Senior High School, Southlake, Texas

Edward Carson

Brooks School, North Andover, Massachusetts

W. W. Norton & Company has been independent since its founding in 1923, when William Warder Norton and Mary D. Herter Norton first published lectures delivered at the People's Institute, the adult education division of New York City's Cooper Union. The firm soon expanded their program beyond the Institute, publishing books by celebrated academics from America and abroad. By midcentury, the two major pillars of Norton's publishing program—trade books and college texts—were firmly established. In the 1950s, the Norton family transferred control of the company to its employees, and today—with a staff of four hundred and a comparable number of trade, college, and professional titles published each year—W. W. Norton & Company stands as the largest and oldest publishing house owned wholly by its employees.

Director of High School Publishing: Jenna Bookin Barry
Project Editor: Melissa Atkin
Editorial Assistant: Aimee Lam
Managing Editor, College: Marian Johnson
Managing Editor, College Digital Media: Kim Yi
Production Manager: Sean Mintus
Composition: Westchester
Manufactured in the United States by RR Donnelley

ISBN 978-0-393-602463 (pbk.)

W. W. Norton & Company, Inc., 500 Fifth Avenue, New York, NY 10110-0017 wwnorton.com

W. W. Norton & Company Ltd., Castle House, 75/76 Wells Street, London WIT 3QT

1 2 3 4 5 6 7 8 9 0

*AP and Advanced Placement program are registered trademarks of the College Board, which was not involved in the production of, and does not endorse, this product. Reprinted by permission of the College Board.

John P. Irish received his B.A. in Philosophy and Political Science, M.A. in Philosophy, and M.L.S. in Humanities from Southern Methodist University, and is currently a Doctorate student in the Humanities program. His current research and dissertation topic are on the role that early nineteenth-century American literature had in shaping the American character. John has been teaching for over 15 years and currently teaches AP U.S. History, American Studies, and Introduction to Philosophy at Carroll Senior High School in Southlake, Texas.

Edward Carson received his B.A. in History and M.Ed. in History Education from Harding University. His current research examines race, religion, and society, particularly that of W.E.B. Du Bois. He does editorial work for *The Christian Century Magazine's Then & Now* section, and sits on the Christian Scholars' Conference Committee. He is a residential faculty member in the History Department at Brooks School in North Andover, Massachusetts.

Contents

Argumentation

Interpretation

Chronological Reasoning

Preface

A Workbook for European History is the second in the series of *Historical Thinking Skills* workbooks. The first in the series, *A Workbook for U.S. History*, garnered attention in high school U.S. History classrooms, particularly because of its alignment with the newly redesigned AP* U.S. History course. We hope that this European History edition will empower teachers and engage students of both regular and AP classes as much as the U.S. History edition did, and we are thankful to all the teachers who shared their enthusiasm and feedback with us during the creation of these two workbooks.

These workbooks offer nine different types of carefully designed graphic organizers, which can be used in a number of different ways. We encourage you to use these graphic organizers to help students conceptualize the specific historical content under investigation in your class. Allow students time to digest the content independently; have them fill in these graphic organizers as notes during a chapter reading on their own; then as a class, ask students to share their thoughts or conclusions. Collaborate as a class to complete the worksheets, not always but often allowing students to interact with their peers while they discuss the topics with each other. Challenge the class by using Socratic questioning to make students think and rethink their positions. Have students challenge each other to incite debates. In fact, there is only one way that we do not want them to be used, and that is by simply handing them out to students, sitting at your desk, and collecting them at the end of the class. The purpose of these workbooks is to get students critically thinking about the historical content in unique and creative ways.

These graphic organizers have helped tremendously to make our classrooms more student-centered. We are becoming facilitators of learning, using these graphic organizers as springboards to get students writing, which is an important step for students to be successful on the AP exams—as well as in college and life. We use these worksheets to assign follow-up or remediation activities for individual students, asking students to develop their own thesis statements based on their conclusions from the worksheets' activities, especially since most of these activities resemble essay prompts from the AP exams. Thus, you can use this workbook as a resource to touch on all three elements of history courses: content, skills, and writing. None of these things exist inside a vacuum, and none are mutually exclusive. In fact, how would someone teach these historical thinking skills without reinforcing the content? How would someone teach writing without reinforcing the content and the relevant skills?

There are a number of folks I would like to continue to thank for all their help and encouragement with these workbooks.

First, Eddie Carson, the co-author of this edition, who agreed to join me in publishing this workbook. His knowledge of European history is impressive and his enthusiasm for this project is much appreciated.

Second, the staff at W. W. Norton & Company, Jenna Barry, Melissa Atkin, Sean Mintus, Aimee Lam, and Christina Illig. Jenna showed continued confidence in me when I approached her with this idea for a second workbook. Melissa has been and continues to be an outstanding editor, even with the addition of a new family member to her immediate family. Sean Mintus, who oversaw the design and production process, was instrumental in helping us make some tight deadlines. Aimee helped us track down original sources for the Interpretation section. Christina spends a tremendous amount of time promoting these books to teachers and school districts around the country. These workbooks would not be here if not for them, their support, hard work, and dedication to bringing the very best resources to teachers. They have been great to work with, and they continue to confirm my decision to sign with Norton for publication of the *Historical Thinking Skills* workbooks.

Third, my students who have tested all of these skills over the past two years as AP U.S. History rolled out its redesign. A number of changes from the U.S. History workbook have been implemented in this European History workbook thanks, in part, to them. My students (past, present, and future) always serve as a source of motivation and encouragement to me and always remind me why I do what I do.

Fourth, my father, Johnny Irish, who was so enthusiastic about the publication of the U.S. History workbook. When things got stressful and I got down, I knew I could always swing by his house and just talk. He always offered me a place to vent, laugh, and cry. His support is essential to anything that I do in life and I cannot thank him enough. He always makes me keep my eye on the big picture, so when things do not go as planned, he is always there to remind me how much my work means to lots of other folks. I care about him more than words can describe.

Fifth, my wife Elizabeth Irish and our immediate family. She continues to show support for me and gives valuable feedback in these projects. Without her support and encouragement this book goes nowhere. Our dog Annie, who constantly reminds me that she exists and needs attention, even when I am really busy, by jumping in my lap, often when I am not expecting it. Our dog Nellie, who reminds me of how much life can and should be taken in strides and lets me know how much fun our walks are, especially when it's just the two of us. And last but not least, our three cats, Tom, Katy, and Lucy. All three chose us as their family, and I cannot imagine how empty life would be without all three of them. This is my immediate family, and it is the best family I could wish for.

To all of these folks I say, thank you!

John P. Irish

I would like to thank my loving parents, Vince and Deloria Carson, who raised me to become a responsible adult. My brother, Michael Carson, for reminding me about the importance of family. And my wife of 20 years, Janette Carson, who places the needs of others before herself.

Eddie Carson

Student Instructions: Causation

When we are asked to identify the historical causation of an event, we are asked to identify the events that led up to the historical event under investigation as well as the results of the historical event under investigation. There can be both long-term and short-term causes and effects. Long-term events are those events that are further away from the historical event under investigation, and short-term events are those events that are more immediate to the historical event under investigation.

The purpose of these Causation activities is to investigate the causes and effects of different events in history. On the surface it may appear easy to identify different causes and effects, however, upon closer examination, it might be surprising to see certain events having stronger causal connections than others. It is also important to practice identifying long-term versus short-term causes and effects and evaluating the most and least important causes and effects of historical events.

Causation: Renaissance (Example)

CAUSE	EFFECT
Crusades Expansion of Mediterranean trade Growth of towns	Printing press Advances in science Religious diversity and change
Geography Skepticism Black Death	Expansion of trade Exploration New political theory
Decline of feudalism Weakening of the Church New wealth	Growth of middle class New monarchs

Most Important and Why?

The expansion of Mediterranean trade extended its connections to Persia and lands of the Orient, which allowed a new class to grow. This class would form the state, thus decreasing papal authority.

Least Important and Why?

Although political theory would promote a level of new thought and state formation found in new monarchs, this rationale had the least impact on the growth of emerging states.

Causation: Renaissance

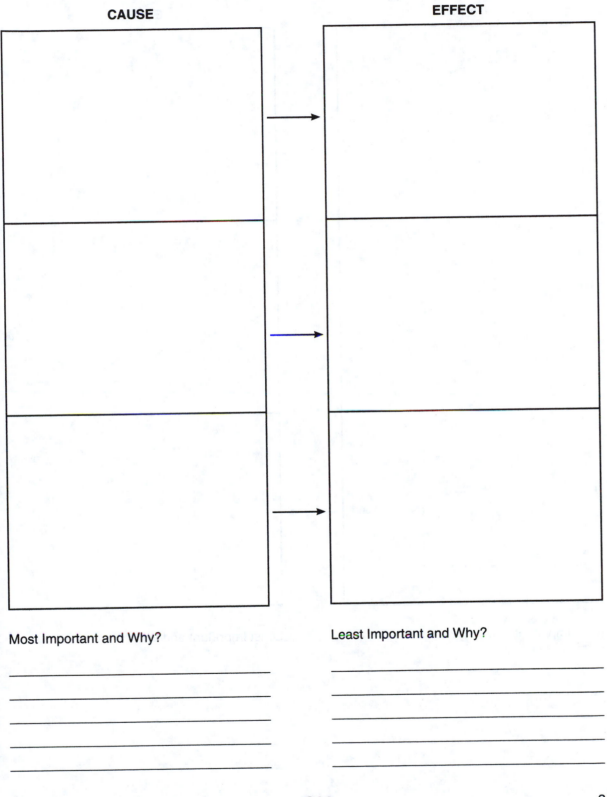

CAUSE   **EFFECT**

Most Important and Why?   Least Important and Why?

_____   _____
_____   _____
_____   _____
_____   _____

Causation: Reformation

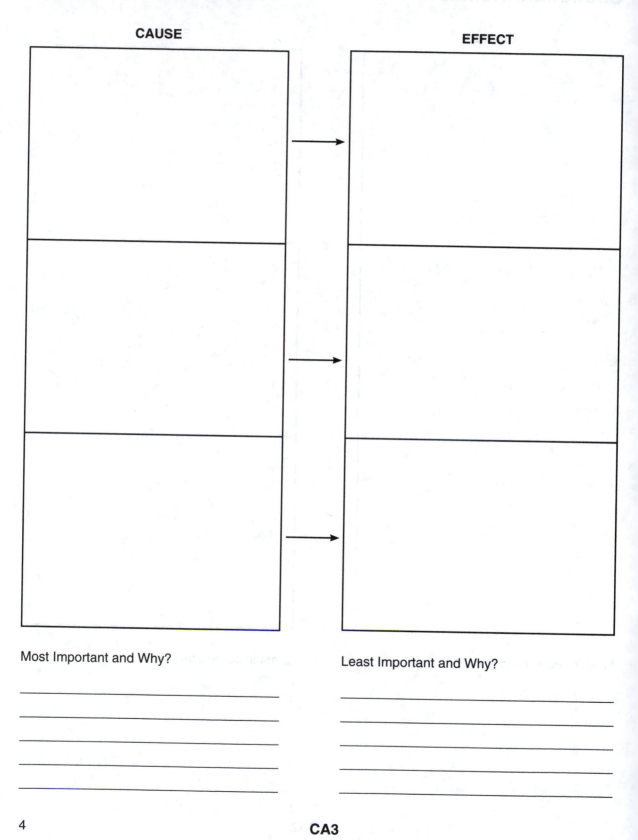

CAUSE

EFFECT

Most Important and Why?

_____
_____
_____
_____
_____

Least Important and Why?

_____
_____
_____
_____
_____

Causation: Rise of an Atlantic Economy

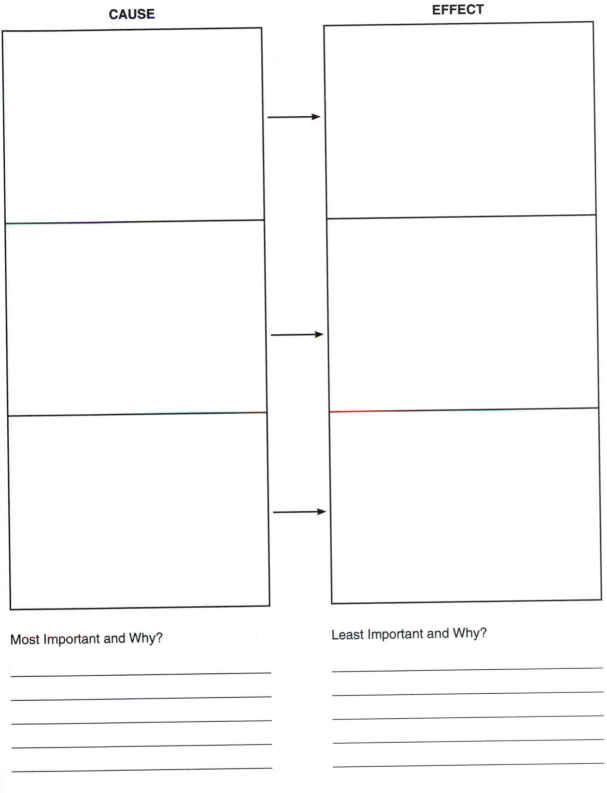

CAUSE

EFFECT

Most Important and Why?

_____
_____
_____
_____
_____

Least Important and Why?

_____
_____
_____
_____
_____

Causation: English Civil War

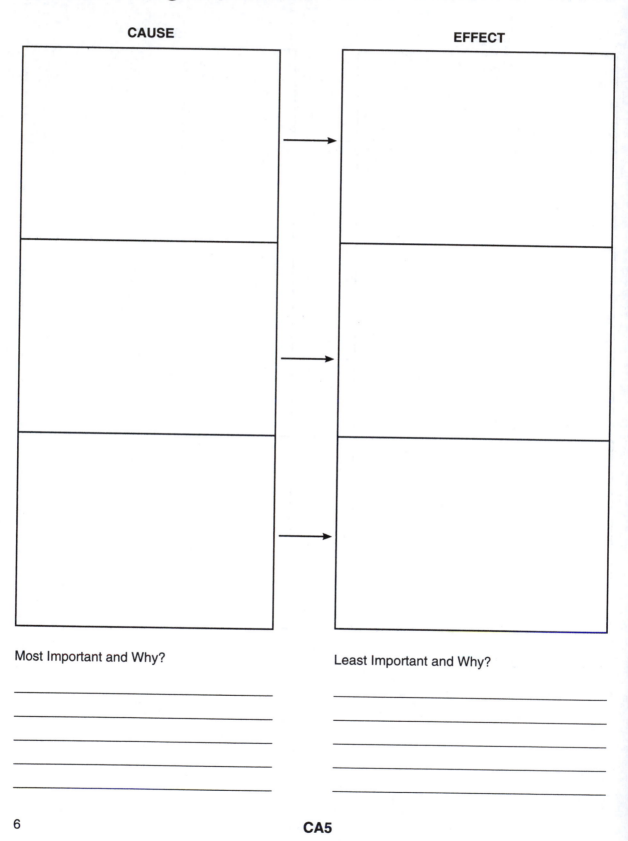

CAUSE

EFFECT

Most Important and Why?

_____
_____
_____
_____
_____

Least Important and Why?

_____
_____
_____
_____
_____

CA5

Causation: Glorious Revolution

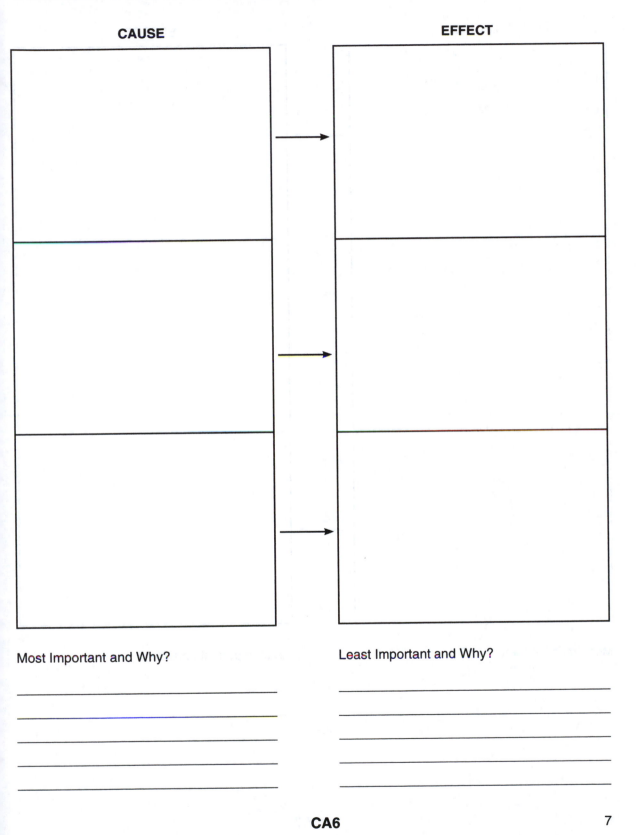

CAUSE

EFFECT

Most Important and Why?

_____
_____
_____
_____
_____

Least Important and Why?

_____
_____
_____
_____
_____

Causation: Rise of the Modern State

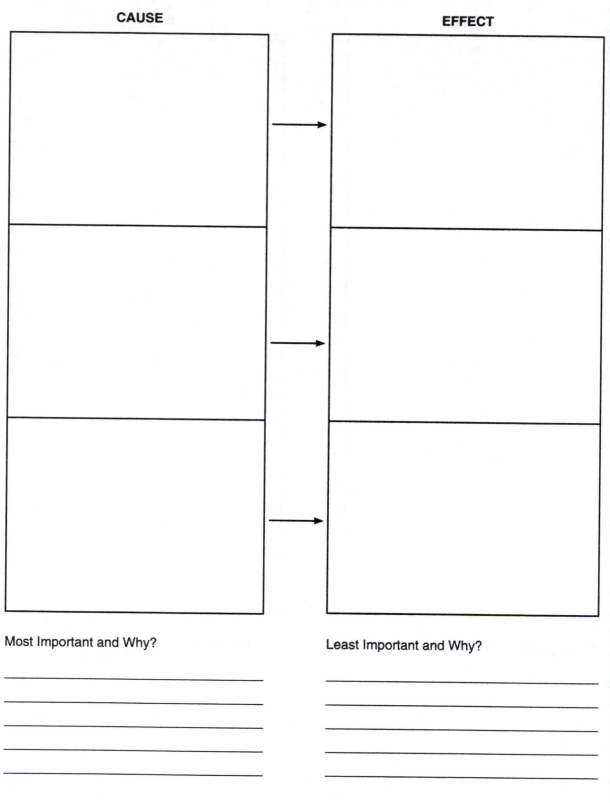

CAUSE

EFFECT

Most Important and Why?

_____
_____
_____
_____
_____

Least Important and Why?

_____
_____
_____
_____
_____

Causation: Scientific Revolution

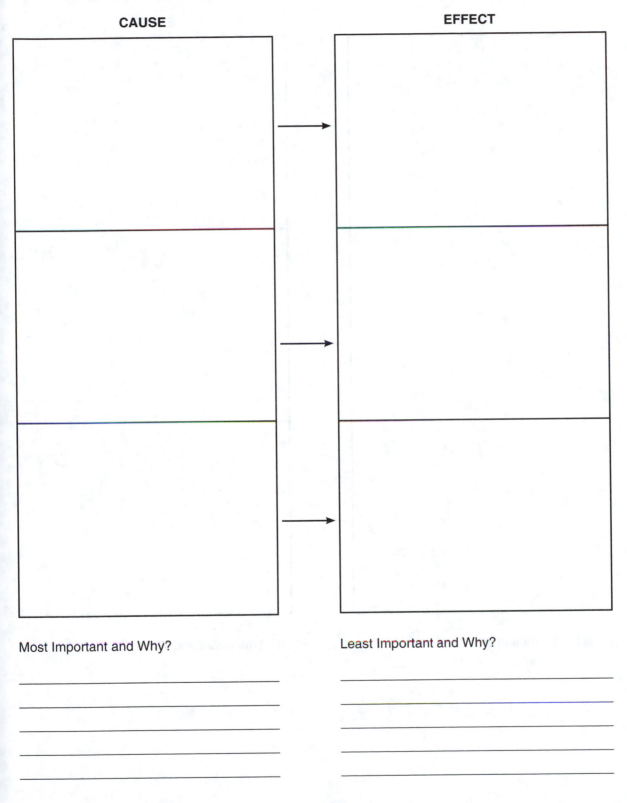

CAUSE

EFFECT

Most Important and Why?

_____
_____
_____
_____
_____

Least Important and Why?

_____
_____
_____
_____
_____

Causation: Enlightenment

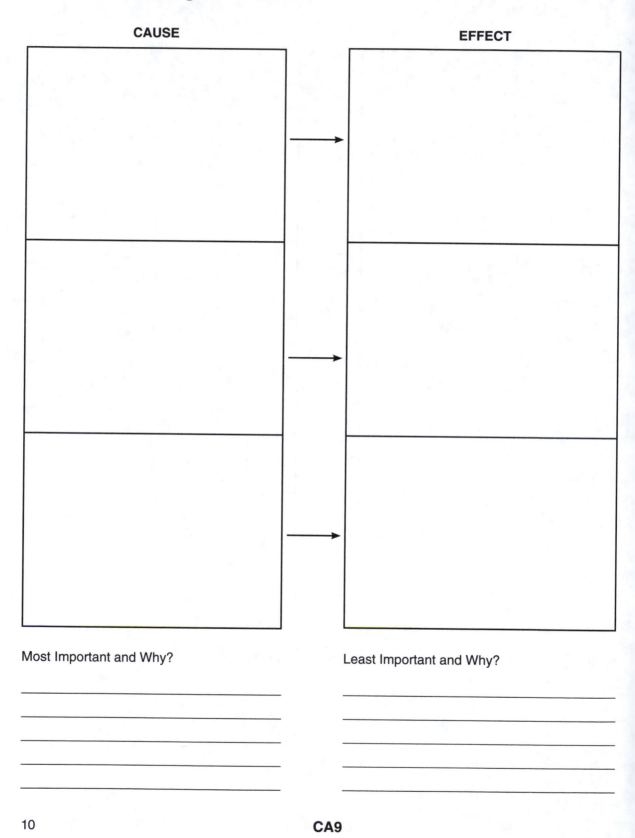

CAUSE

EFFECT

Most Important and Why?

_____
_____
_____
_____
_____

Least Important and Why?

_____
_____
_____
_____
_____

CA9

Causation: Industrial Revolution

CAUSE   **EFFECT**

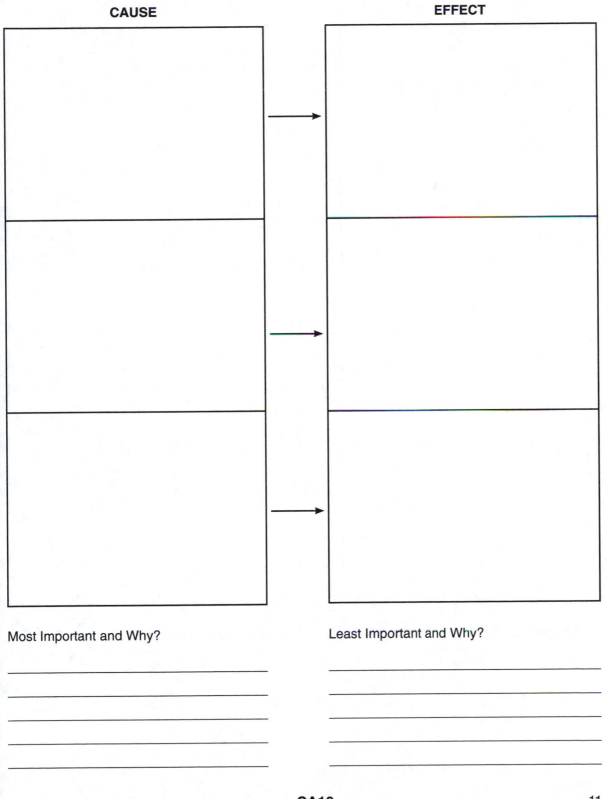

Most Important and Why?   Least Important and Why?

_____   _____

_____   _____

_____   _____

_____   _____

_____   _____

Causation: Growth of Towns / Cities

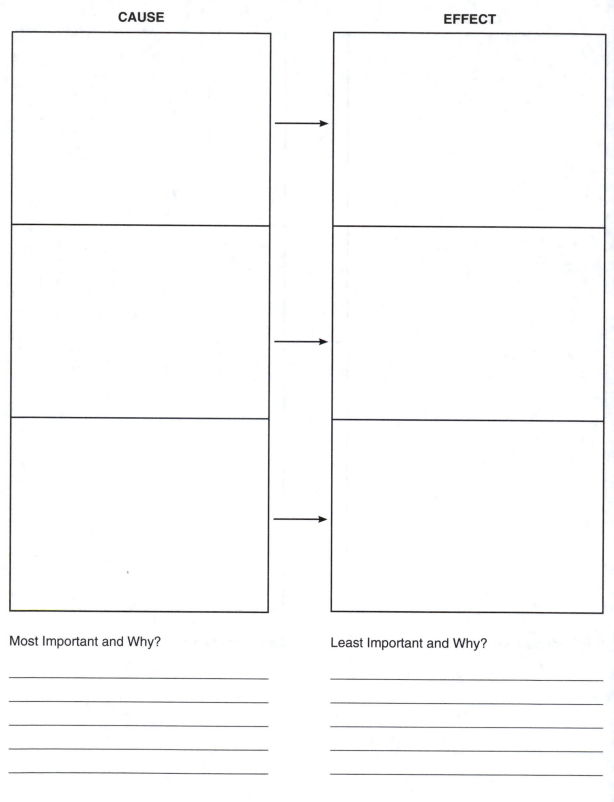

CAUSE

EFFECT

Most Important and Why?

_____

_____

_____

_____

_____

Least Important and Why?

_____

_____

_____

_____

_____

Causation: Rise of British Nationalism

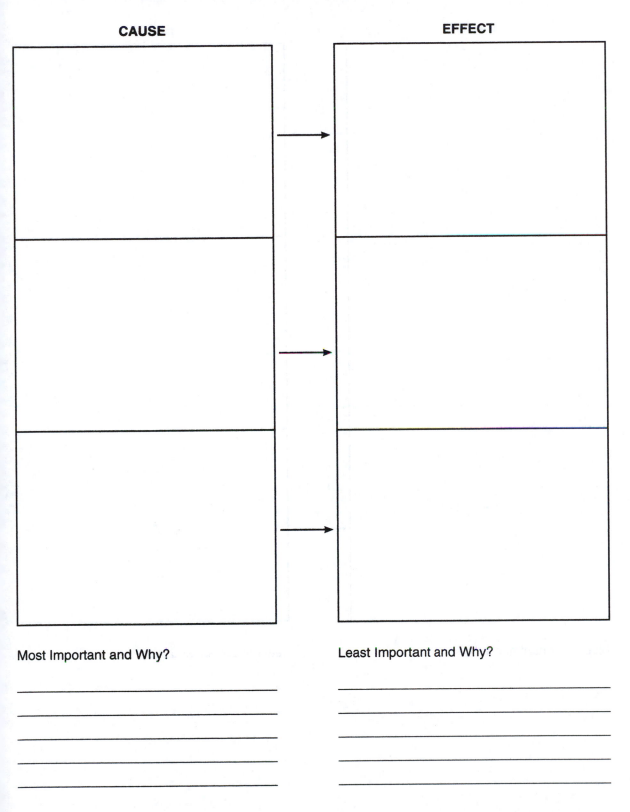

CAUSE   EFFECT

Most Important and Why?   Least Important and Why?

_____   _____
_____   _____
_____   _____
_____   _____
_____   _____

Causation: French Revolution

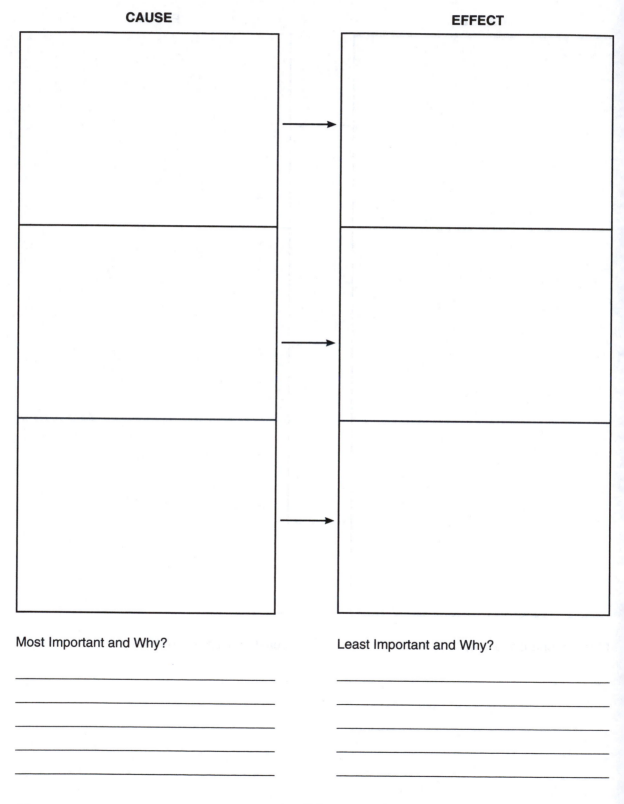

CAUSE

EFFECT

Most Important and Why?

_____
_____
_____
_____
_____

Least Important and Why?

_____
_____
_____
_____
_____

Causation: Napoleon

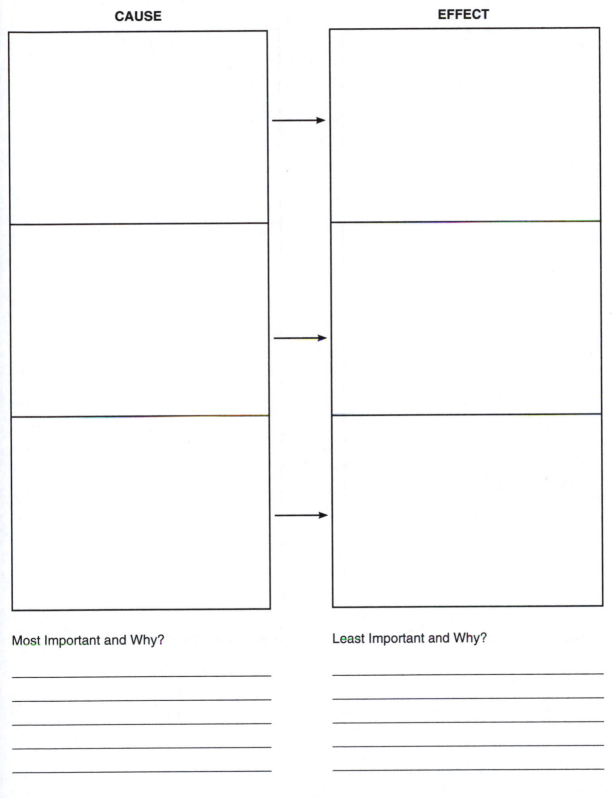

CAUSE

EFFECT

Most Important and Why?

_____

_____

_____

_____

_____

Least Important and Why?

_____

_____

_____

_____

_____

Causation: Romantic Movement

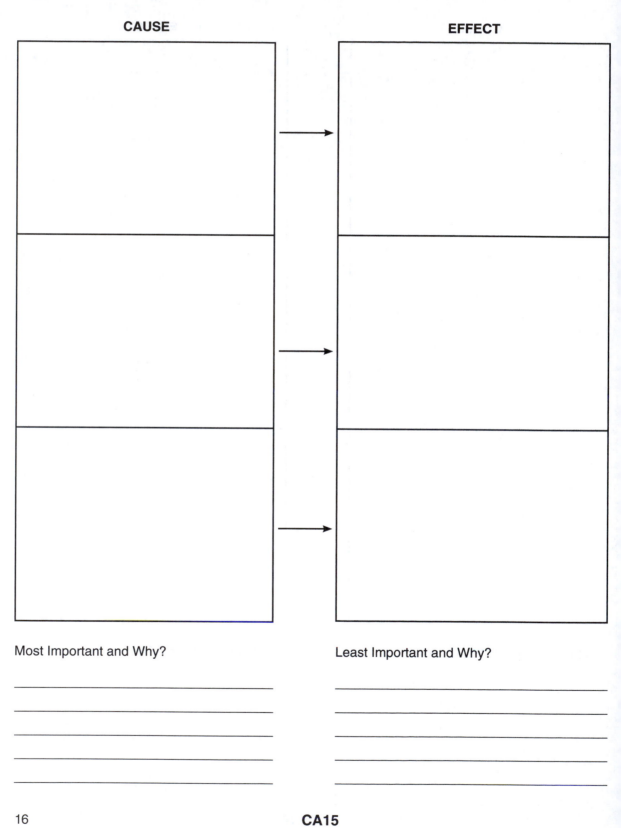

CAUSE

EFFECT

Most Important and Why?

_____

_____

_____

_____

_____

Least Important and Why?

_____

_____

_____

_____

_____

Causation: Revolutions of 1848

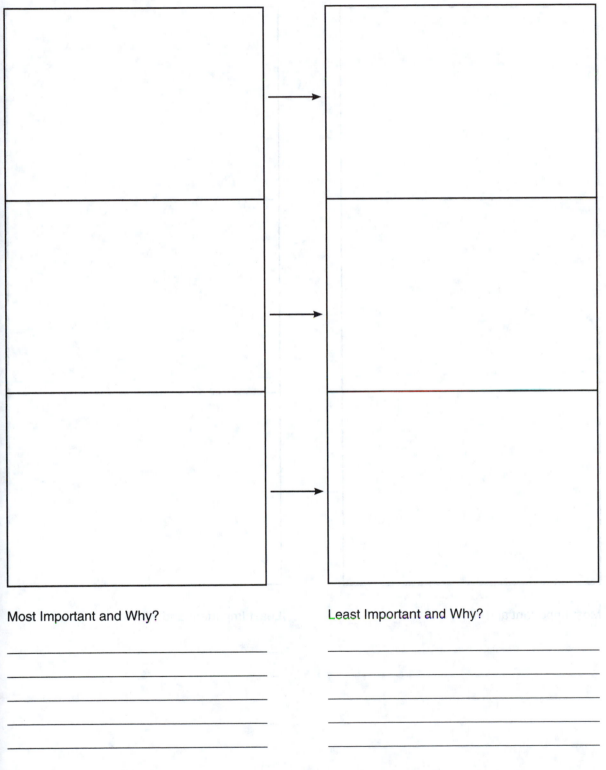

CAUSE

EFFECT

Most Important and Why?

_____

_____

_____

_____

_____

Least Important and Why?

_____

_____

_____

_____

_____

Causation: Age of Realism

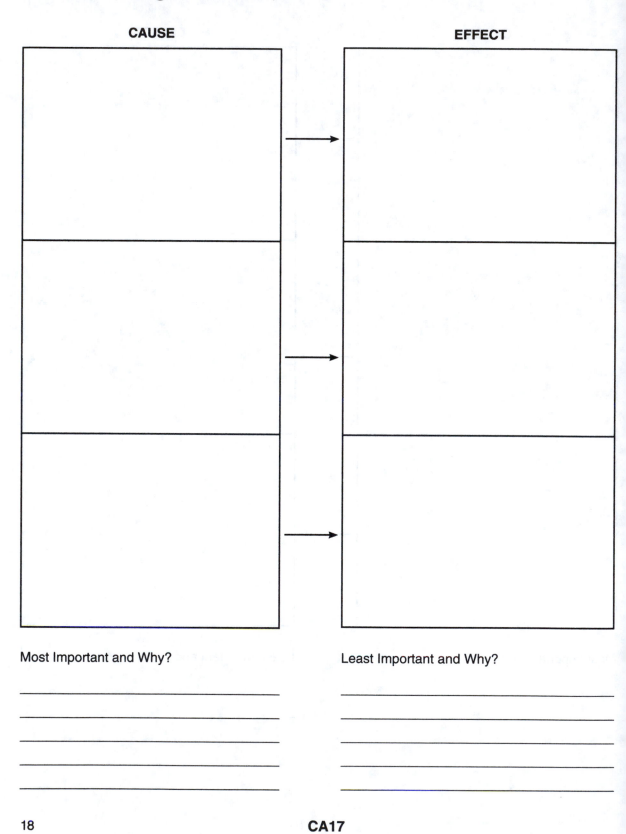

CAUSE   EFFECT

Most Important and Why?

_____
_____
_____
_____
_____

Least Important and Why?

_____
_____
_____
_____
_____

Causation: 19th-Century State Reforms

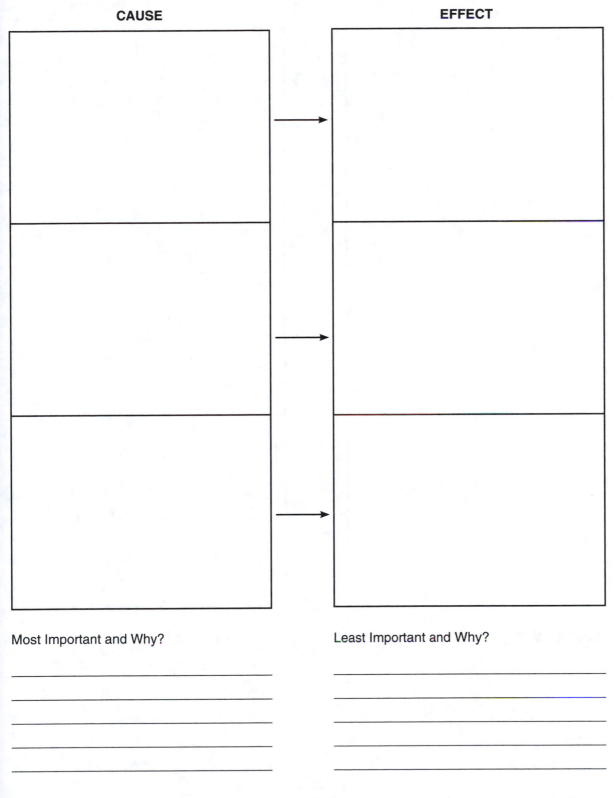

CAUSE

EFFECT

Most Important and Why?

_____
_____
_____
_____
_____

Least Important and Why?

_____
_____
_____
_____
_____

Causation: German and Italian Unifications

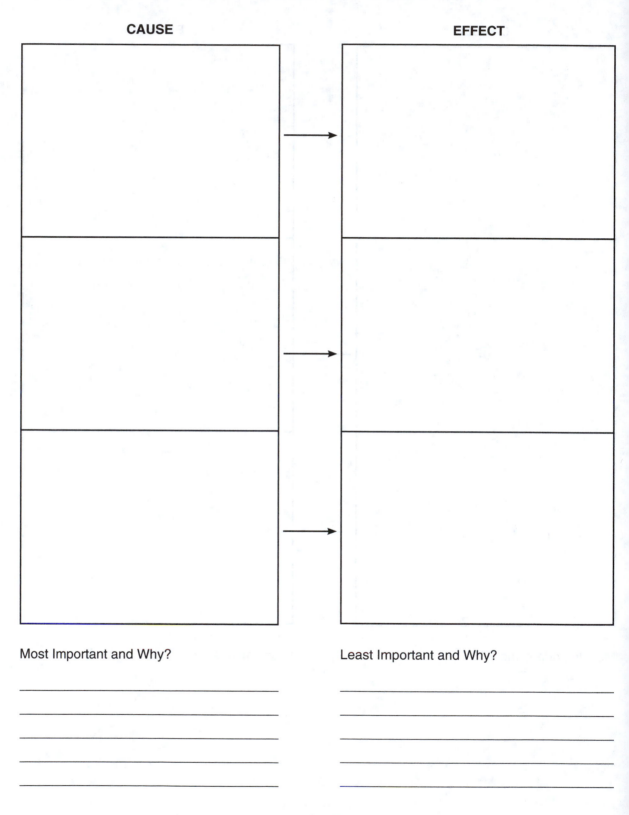

CAUSE   EFFECT

Most Important and Why?

_____
_____
_____
_____
_____

Least Important and Why?

_____
_____
_____
_____
_____

         CA19

Causation: End of Russian Serfdom

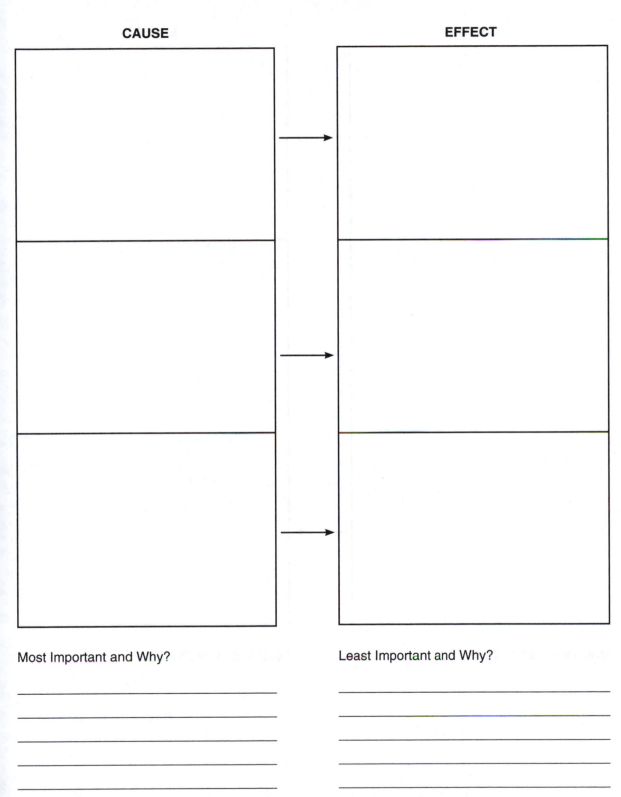

CAUSE

EFFECT

Most Important and Why?

_____

_____

_____

_____

_____

Least Important and Why?

_____

_____

_____

_____

_____

Causation: Second Industrial Revolution

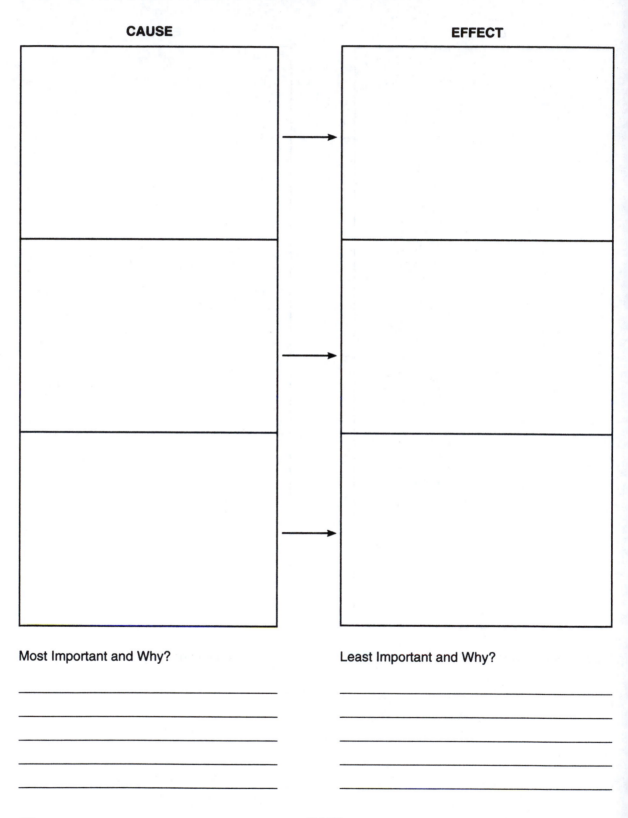

CAUSE

EFFECT

Most Important and Why?

_____
_____
_____
_____
_____

Least Important and Why?

_____
_____
_____
_____
_____

Causation: New Imperialism

CAUSE		EFFECT

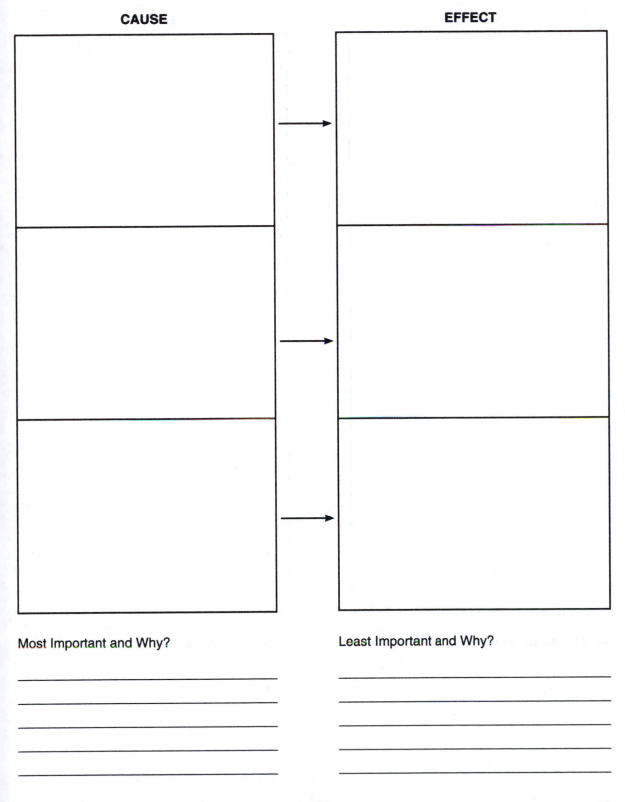

Most Important and Why?

_____

_____

_____

_____

_____

Least Important and Why?

_____

_____

_____

_____

_____

Causation: World War I

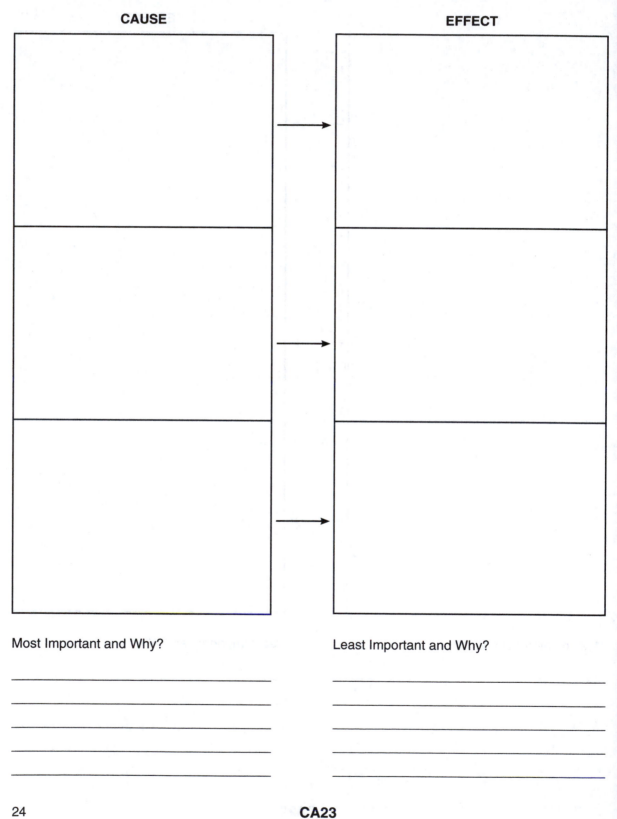

CAUSE

EFFECT

Most Important and Why?

_____
_____
_____
_____
_____

Least Important and Why?

_____
_____
_____
_____

Causation: Russian Revolution

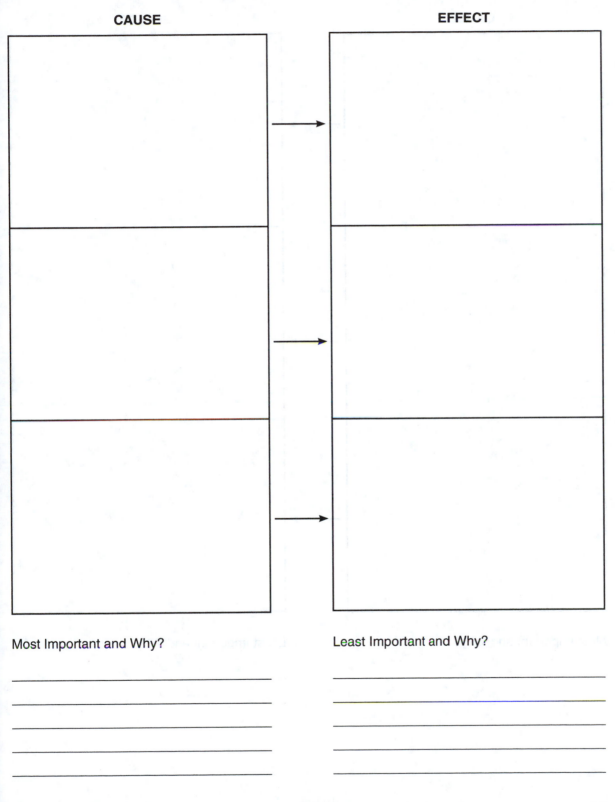

CAUSE	EFFECT

Most Important and Why?

_____
_____
_____
_____
_____

Least Important and Why?

_____
_____
_____
_____
_____

Causation: Great Depression

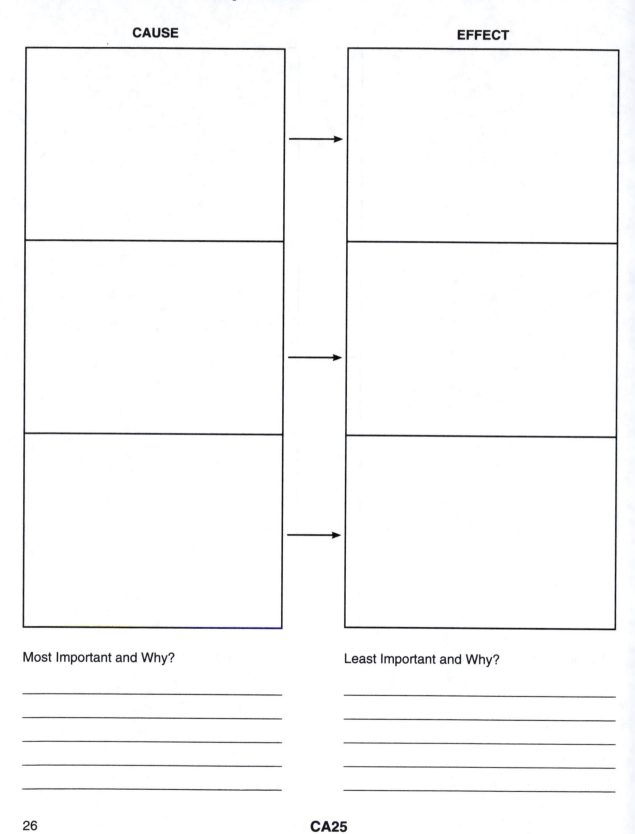

CAUSE   EFFECT

Most Important and Why?

_____

_____

_____

_____

_____

Least Important and Why?

_____

_____

_____

_____

_____

Causation: World War II

CAUSE		EFFECT

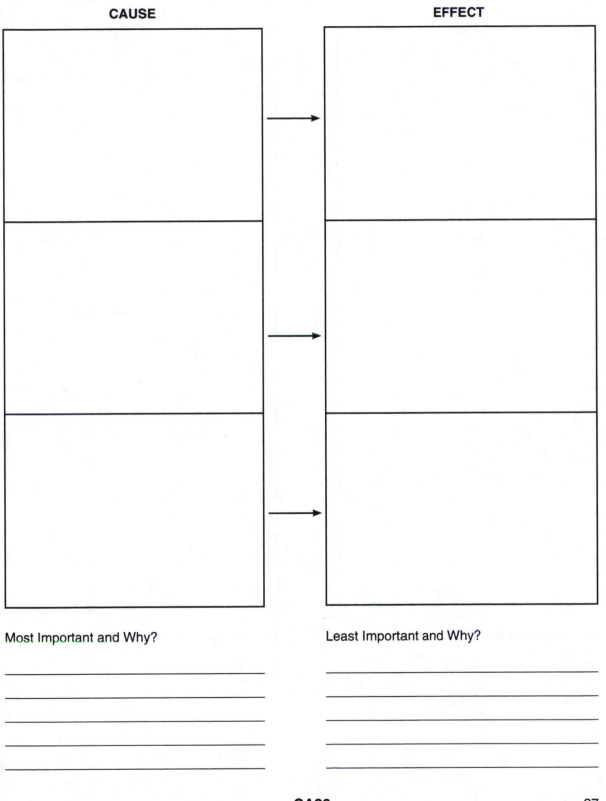

Most Important and Why?

_____

_____

_____

_____

_____

Least Important and Why?

_____

_____

_____

_____

_____

Causation: Cold War

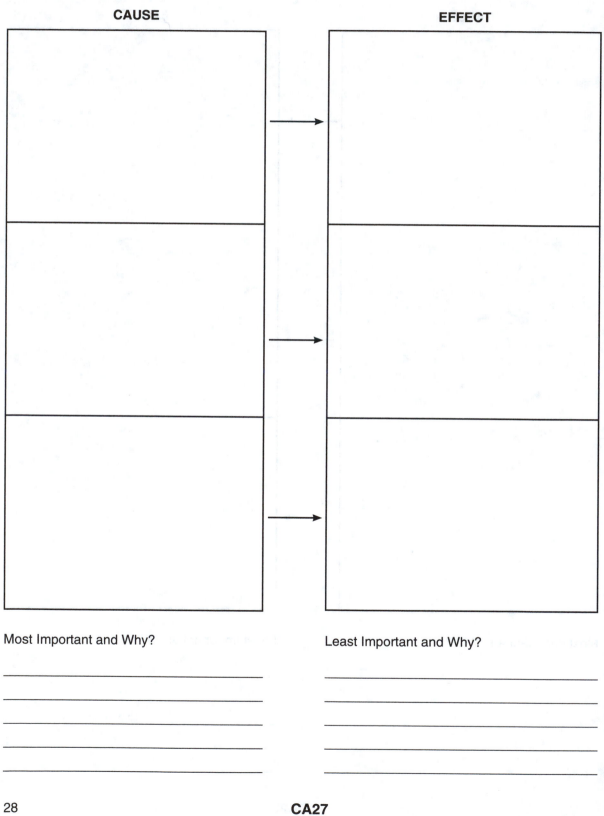

CAUSE

EFFECT

Most Important and Why?

_____
_____
_____
_____
_____

Least Important and Why?

_____
_____
_____
_____
_____

Causation: Decolonization

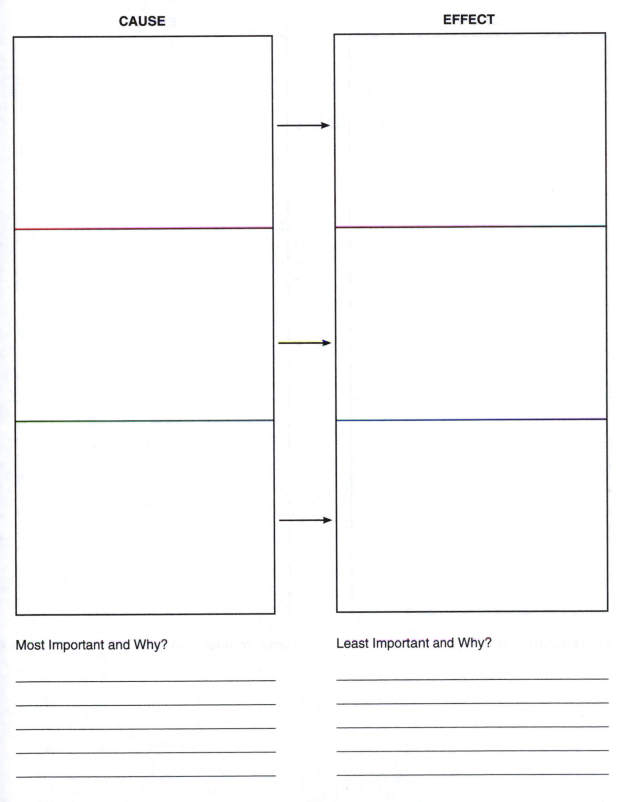

CAUSE	EFFECT

Most Important and Why?

_____
_____
_____
_____
_____

Least Important and Why?

_____
_____
_____
_____
_____

Causation: Green Revolution

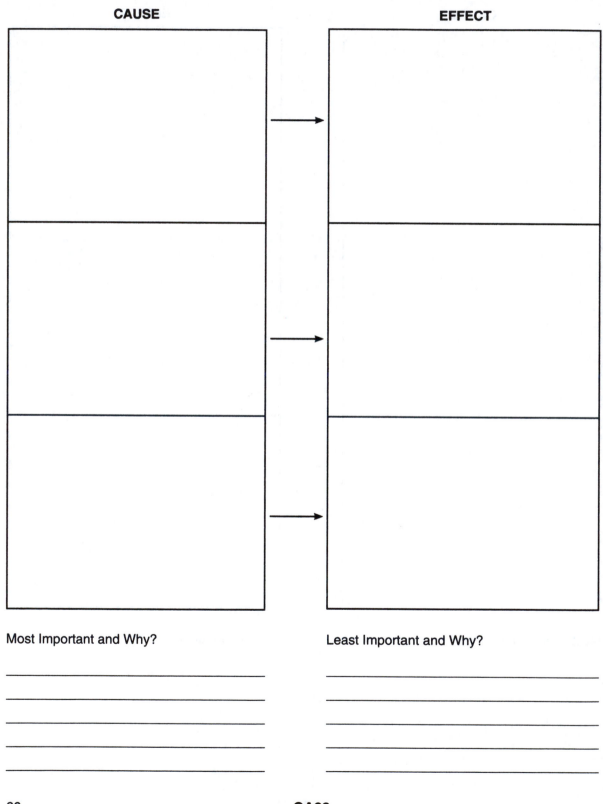

CAUSE

EFFECT

Most Important and Why?

_____
_____
_____
_____
_____

Least Important and Why?

_____
_____
_____
_____
_____

Causation: Collapse of the Berlin Wall

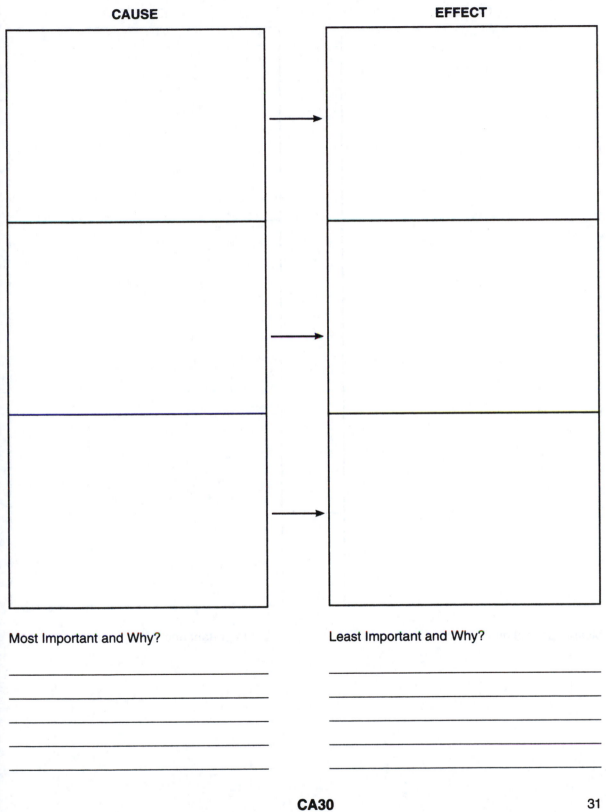

CAUSE

EFFECT

Most Important and Why?

_____

_____

_____

_____

_____

Least Important and Why?

_____

_____

_____

_____

_____

Causation: Fall of Communism in the USSR

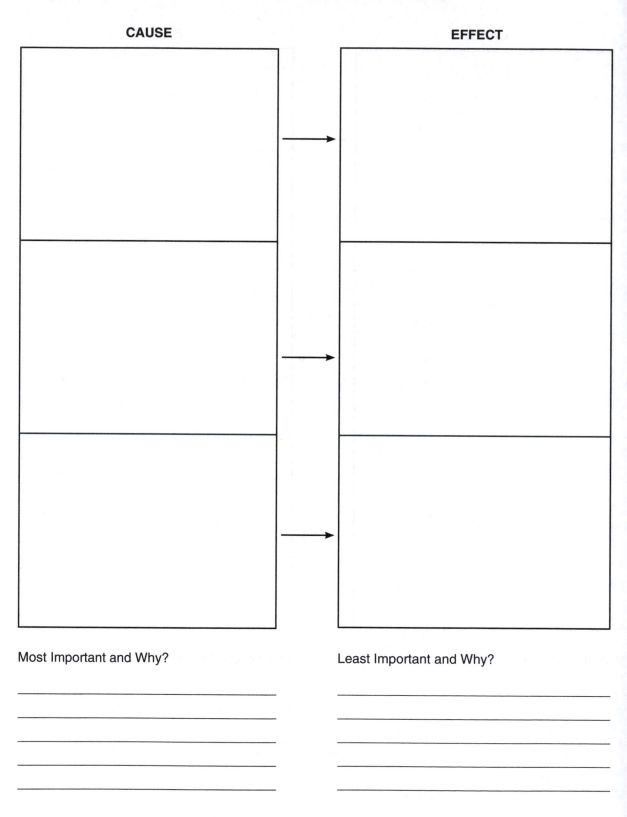

CAUSE

EFFECT

Most Important and Why?

_____
_____
_____
_____
_____

Least Important and Why?

_____
_____
_____
_____
_____

CA31

Student Instructions: Comparison

When we are asked to compare things, we are asked to identify similarities and differences among the different things under consideration. Similarities are the things that they have in common, that is, the things that are shared between the two entities. Differences are the things that are unique to that particular entity; in some cases, these can be things that are contradictory with other characteristics.

The purpose of these Comparison activities is to analyze how similar and different certain historical topics are within their historical contexts. On the surface, it may appear that different topics have no similarities or differences; but upon further inspection, we often see that, indeed, many historical topics are more complex than we realized. But recognizing the similarities and differences is only the beginning of these activities' purpose. They ask us to dig deeper into our observations and to move from observation to evaluation. We should evaluate *why* there are similarities and differences between the two historical topics.

Comparison: Italian Renaissance and Northern Renaissance (Example)

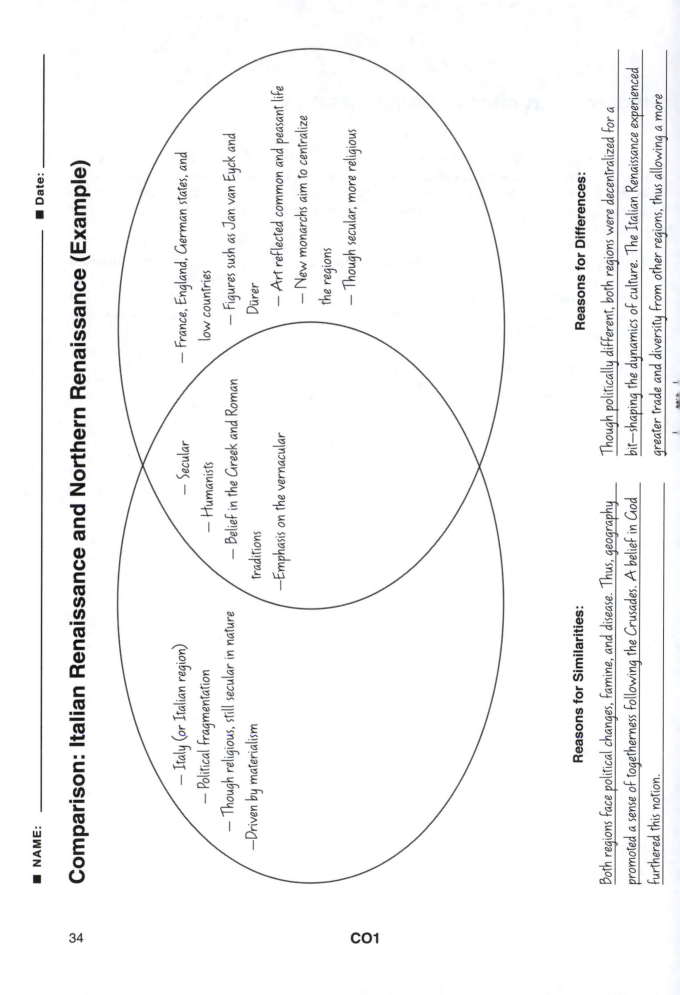

— Italy (or Italian region)
— Political fragmentation
— Though religious, still secular in nature
—Driven by materialism

— Secular
— Humanists
— Belief in the Greek and Roman traditions
—Emphasis on the vernacular

— France, England, German states, and low countries
— Figures sush as Jan van Eyck and Dürer
— Art reflected common and peasant life
— New monarchs aim to centralize the regions
— Though secular, more religious

Reasons for Similarities:

Both regions face political changes, famine, and disease. Thus, geography promoted a sense of togetherness following the Crusades. A belief in God furthered this notion.

Reasons for Differences:

Though politically different, both regions were decentralized for a bit—shaping the dynamics of culture. The Italian Renaissance experienced greater trade and diversity from other regions, thus allowing a more

CO1

Comparison: Italian Renaissance and Northern Renaissance

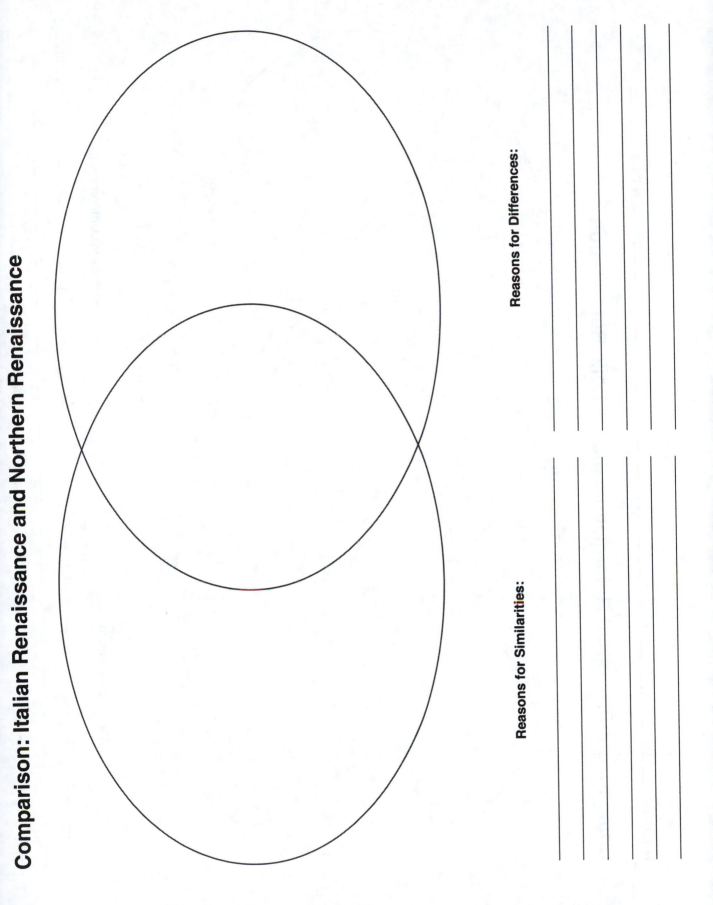

Reasons for Differences:

Reasons for Similarities:

Comparison: Protestant Reformation and Catholic Reformation

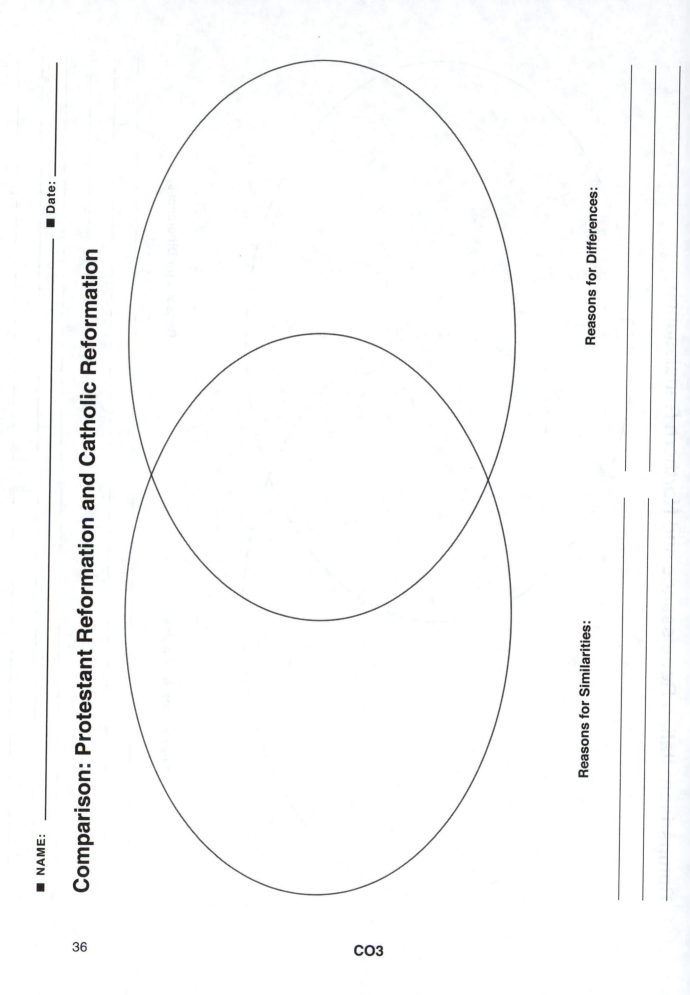

Reasons for Differences:
_____
_____
_____

Reasons for Similarities:
_____
_____
_____

CO3

Comparison: Lutheranism and Calvinism

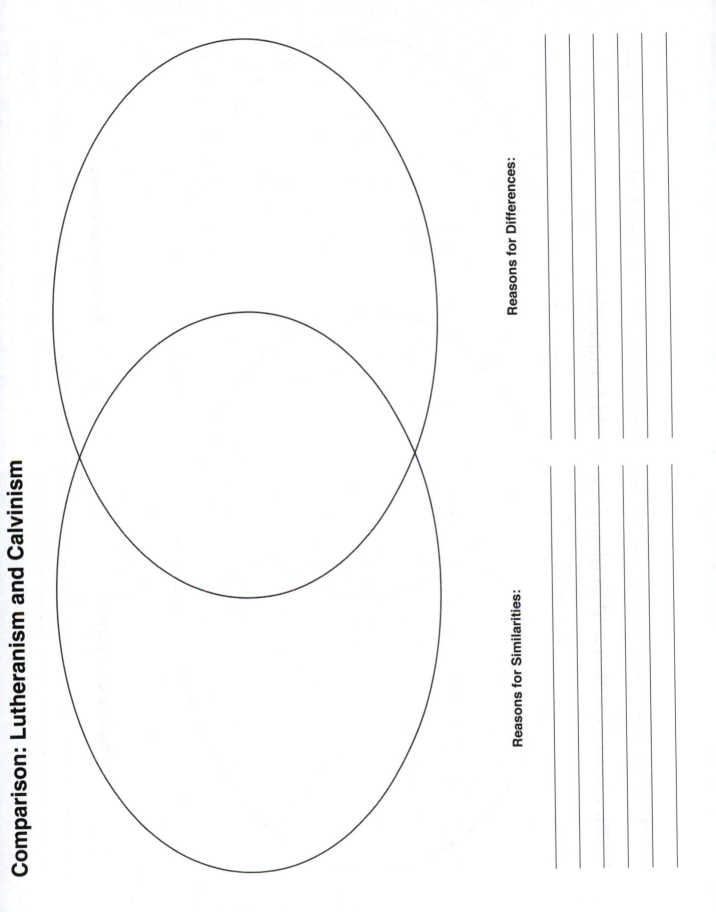

Reasons for Differences:

Reasons for Similarities:

Comparison: Spanish and English New World Conquests

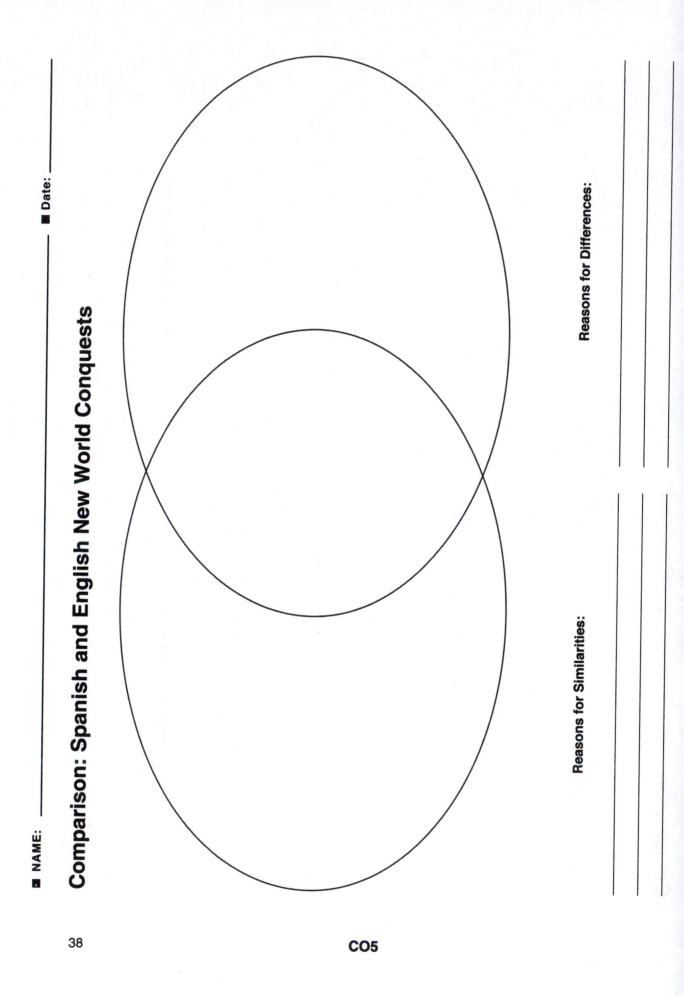

Reasons for Differences:

Reasons for Similarities:

Comparison: English Reformation and German Reformation

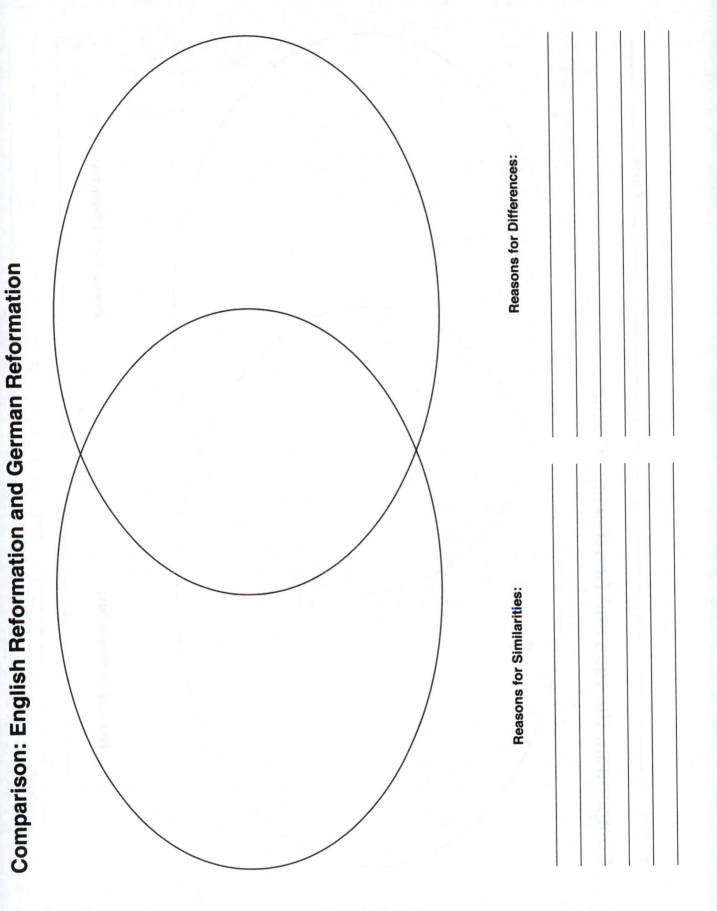

Reasons for Differences:

Reasons for Similarities:

Comparison: Baroque and Renaissance Cultures

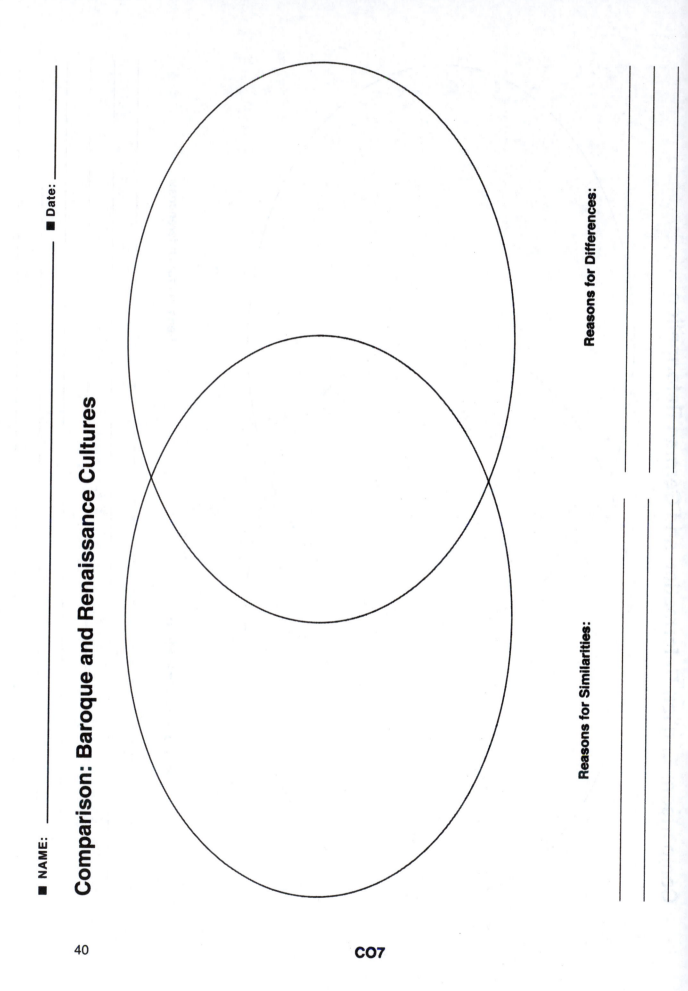

Reasons for Similarities:

Reasons for Differences:

40

Comparison: Treaty of Augsburg and Peace of Westphalia

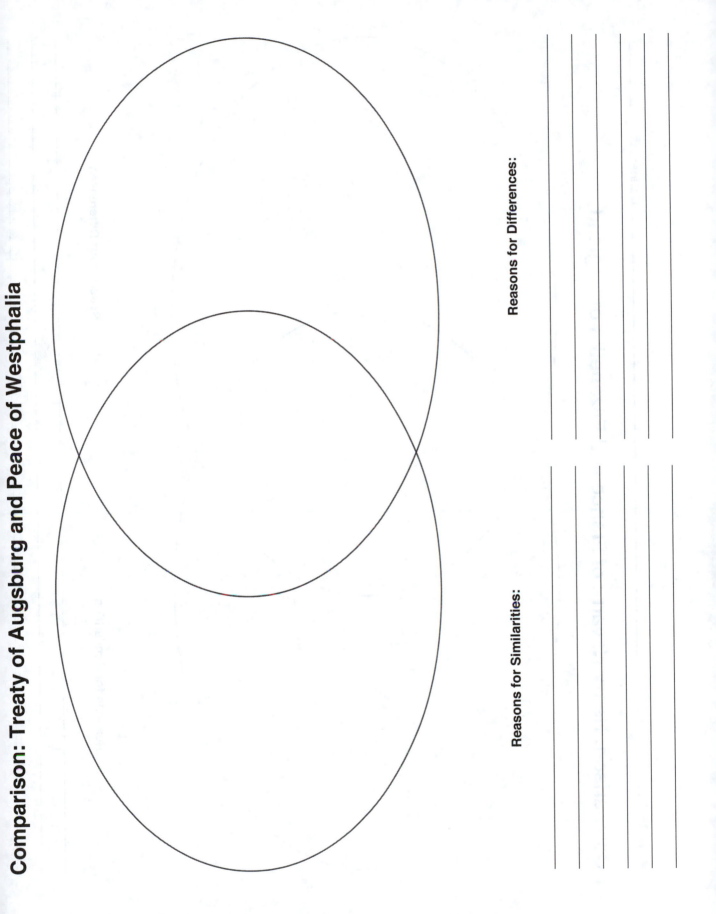

Reasons for Differences:

Reasons for Similarities:

Comparison: Henry Navarre of France and Elizabeth I of England

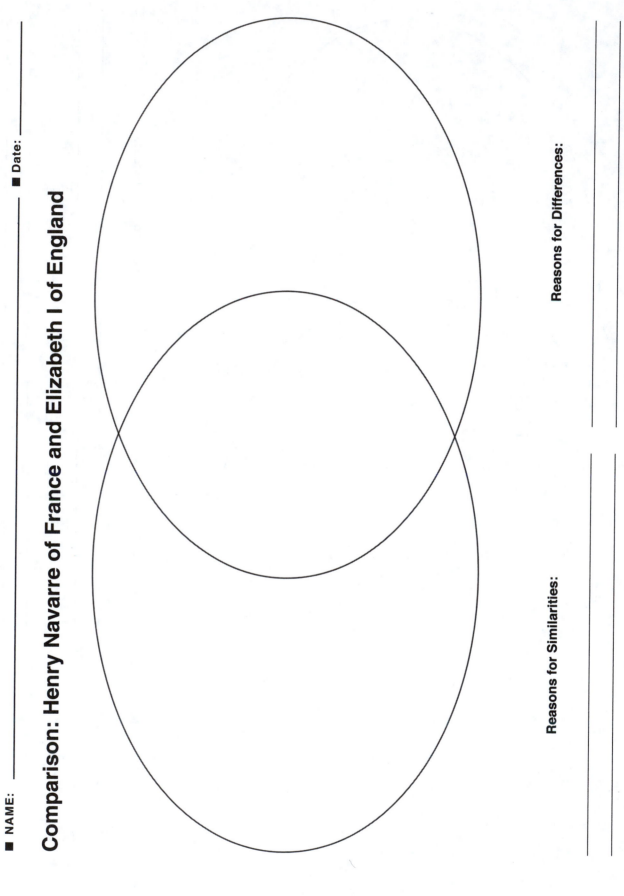

Reasons for Differences:

_____

_____

_____

Reasons for Similarities:

_____

_____

_____

42   **CO9**

Comparison: Rise and Decline of Spain and the Dutch Republic

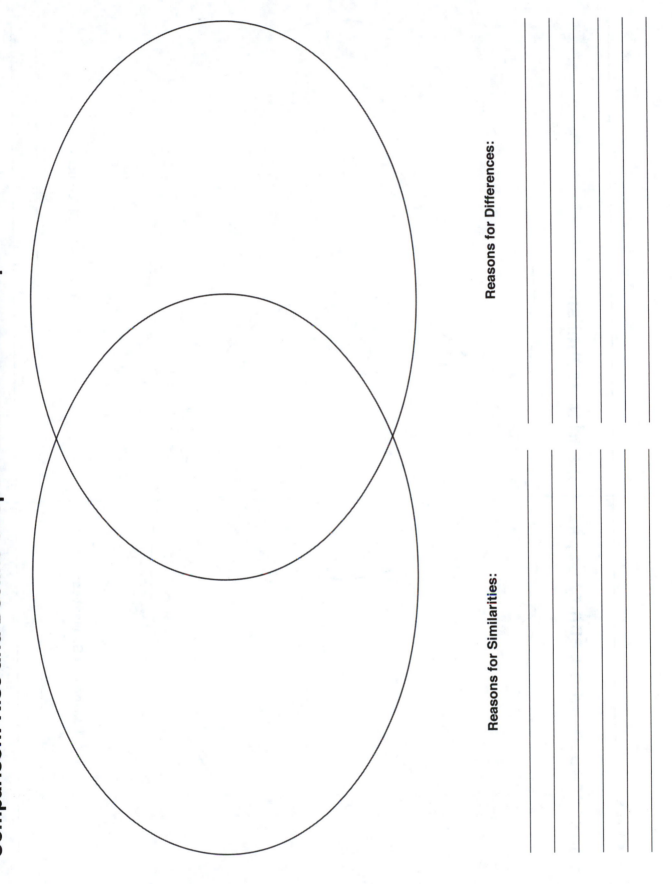

Reasons for Differences:

Reasons for Similarities:

Comparison: 18th-Century Capitalism and Mercantilism

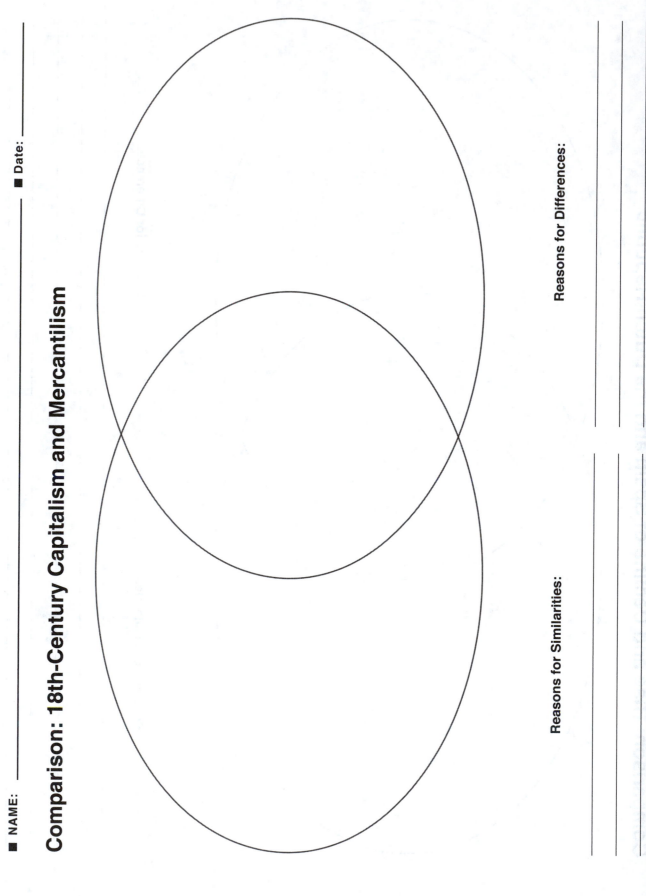

Reasons for Differences:

Reasons for Similarities:

CO11

Comparison: Western and Eastern Absolutism

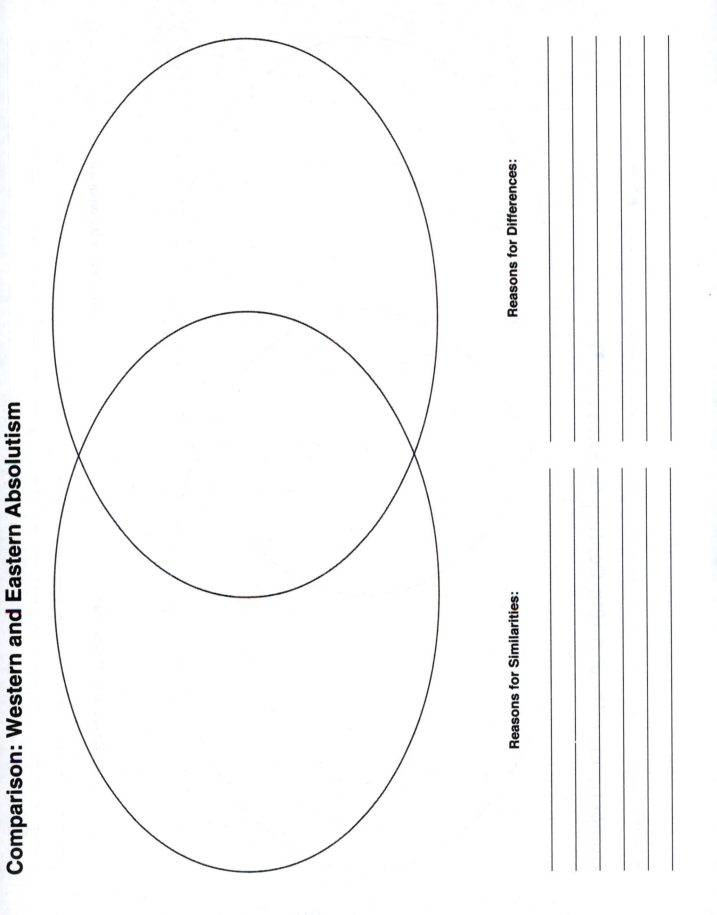

Reasons for Differences:

Reasons for Similarities:

Comparison: 17th- and 19th-Century Science and Thought

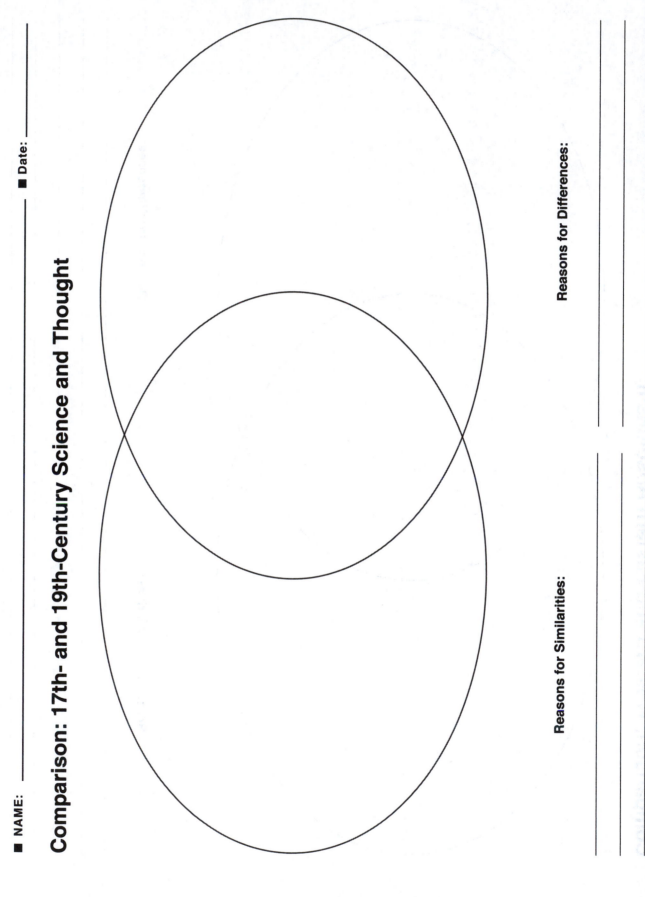

Reasons for Differences:

Reasons for Similarities:

Comparison: French and Spanish Inquisitions

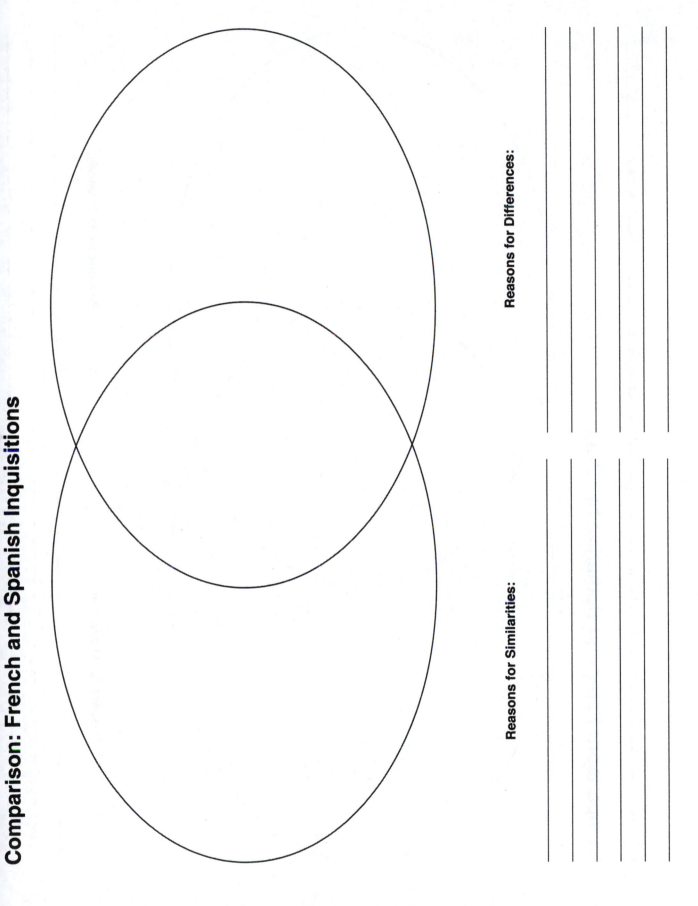

Reasons for Differences:

Reasons for Similarities:

Comparison: Peter and Catherine the Great

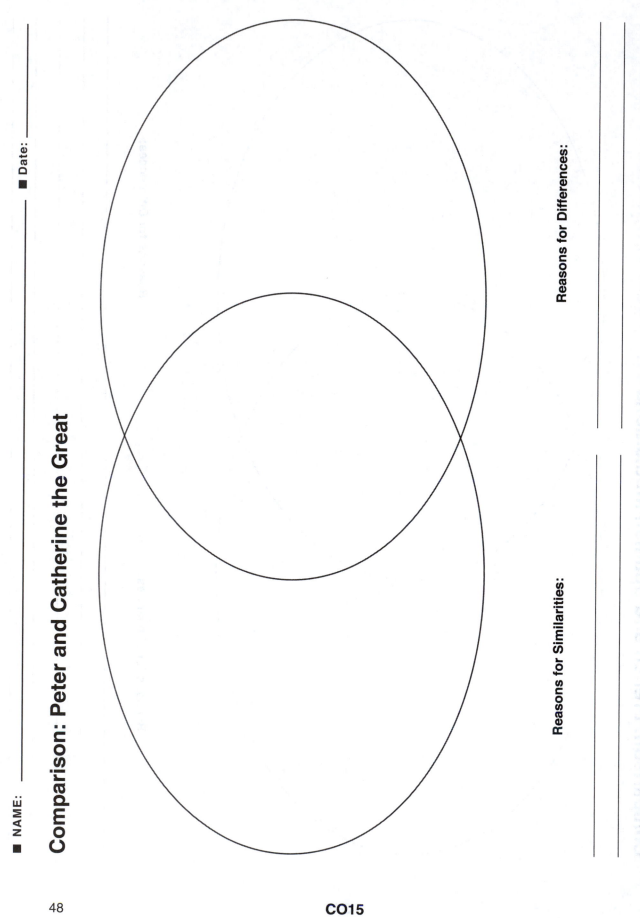

Reasons for Differences:

Reasons for Similarities:

CO15

Comparison: Joseph II of Austria and Frederick the Great of Prussia

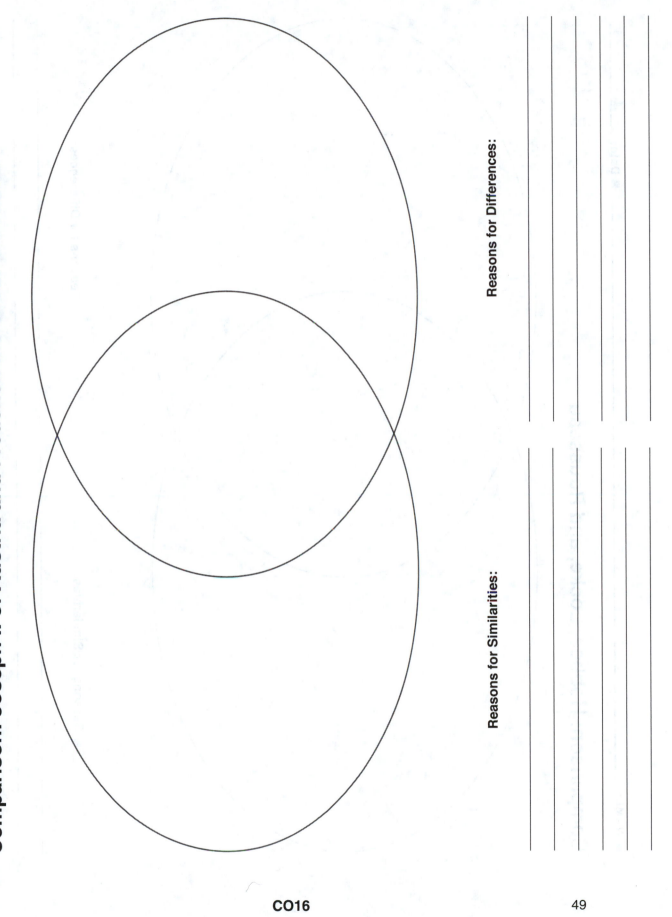

Reasons for Differences:

Reasons for Similarities:

Comparison: Hobbes, Locke, and Rousseau

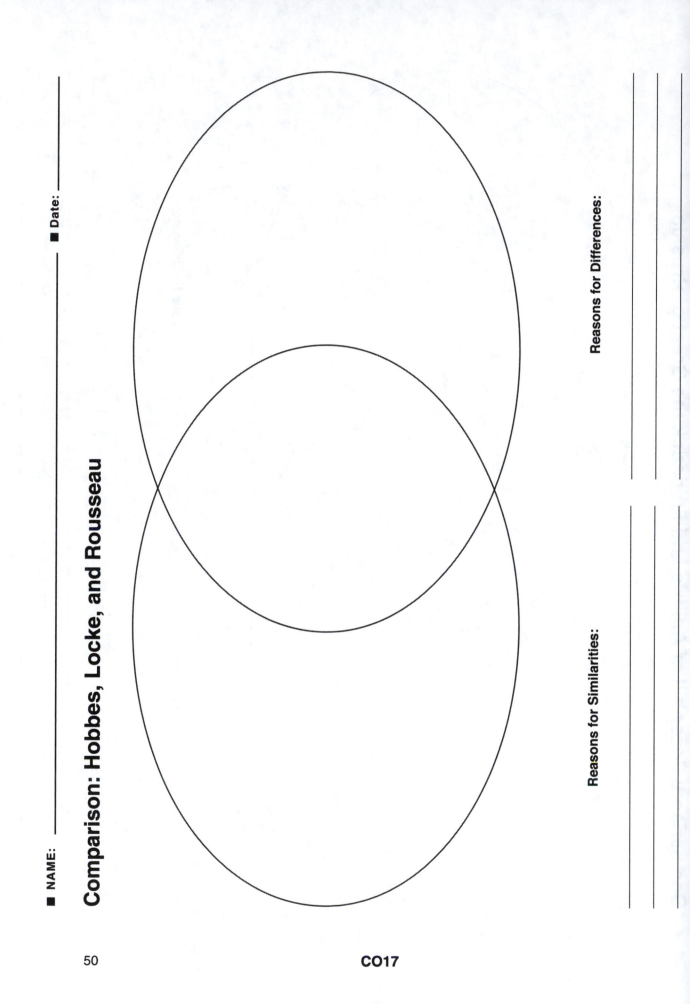

Reasons for Differences:

Reasons for Similarities:

CO17

Comparison: German and Italian Unifications

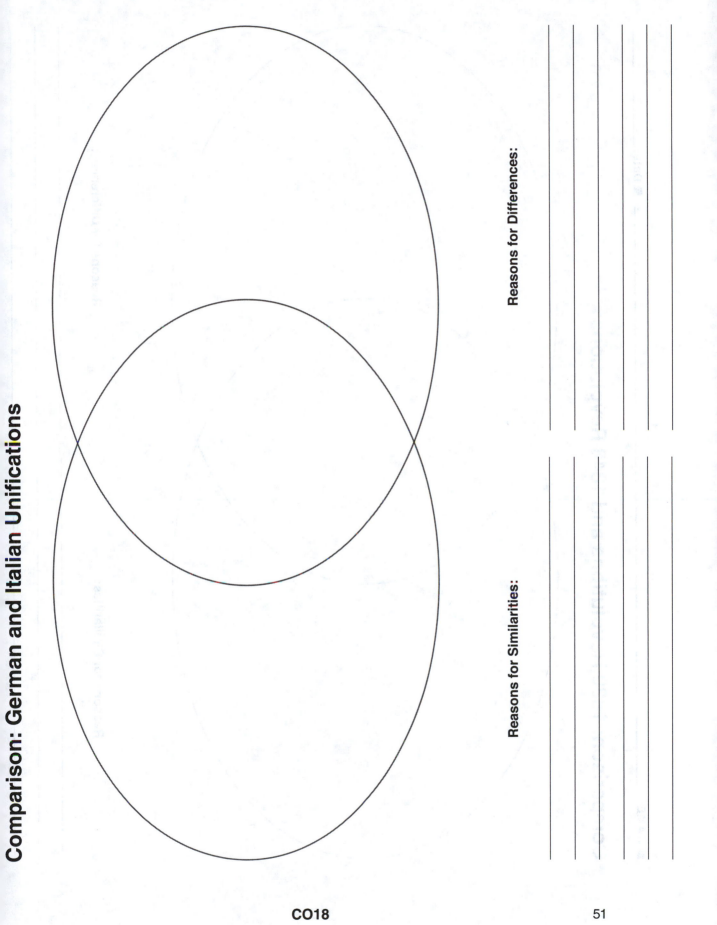

Reasons for Differences:

Reasons for Similarities:

Comparison: 1830 Revolutions and 1848 Revolutions

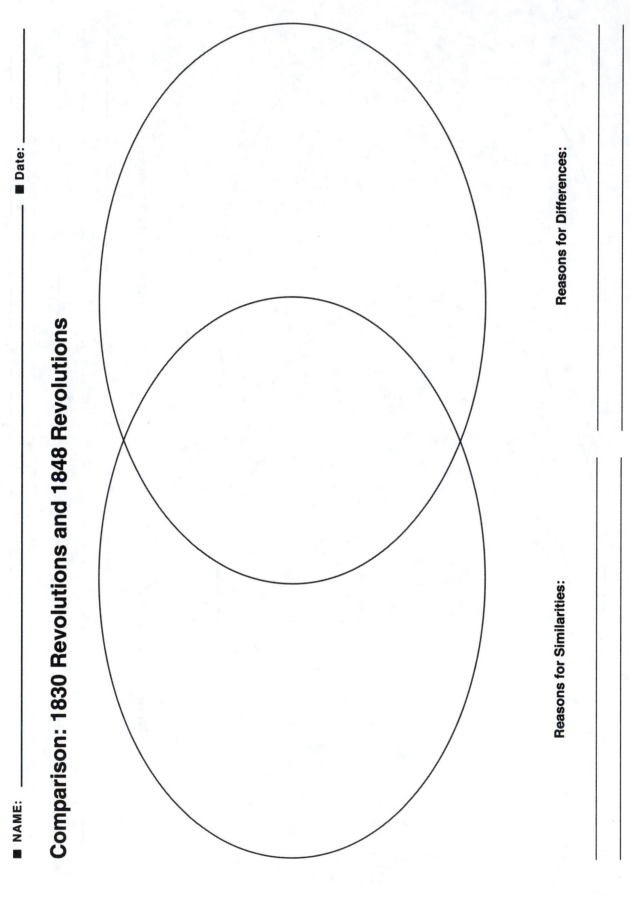

Reasons for Differences:

_____

_____

Reasons for Similarities:

_____

_____

Comparison: Anarchists and Syndicalists

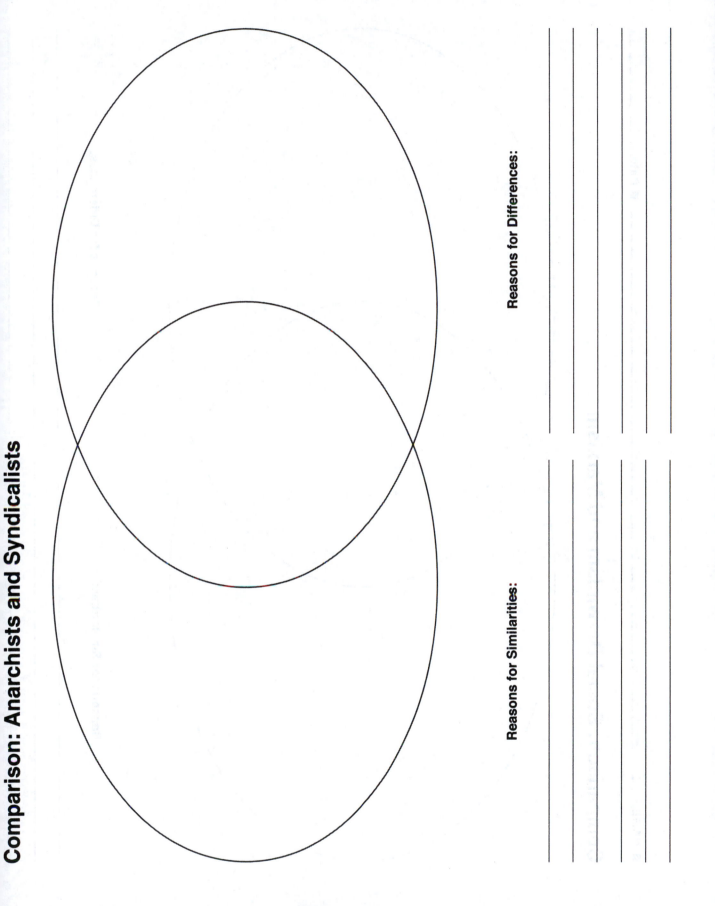

Reasons for Differences:

Reasons for Similarities:

Comparison: Social Darwinism and Marxism

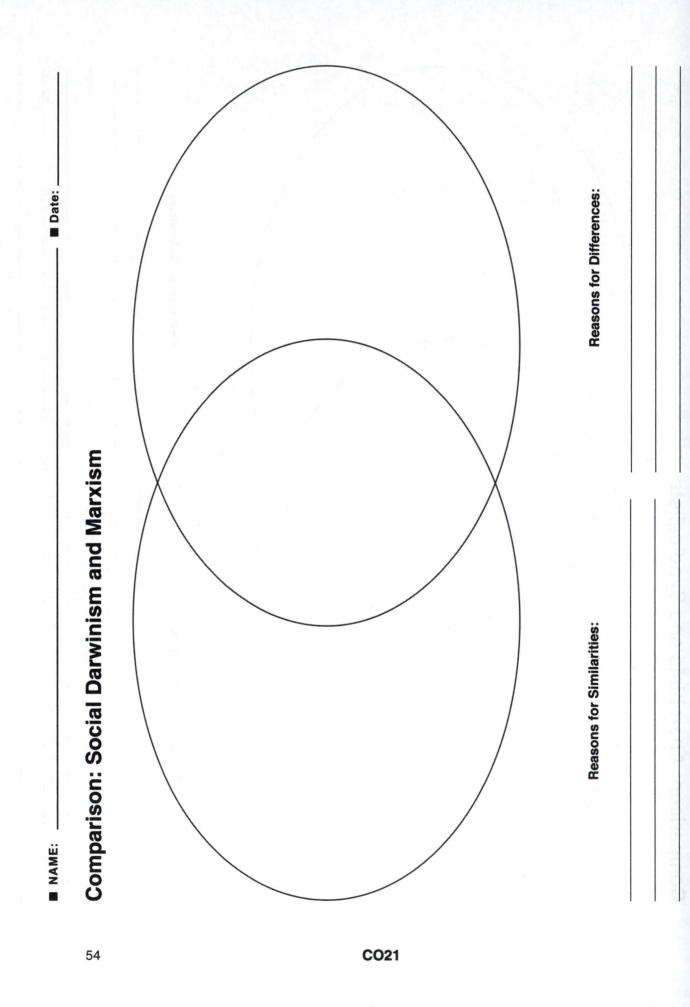

Reasons for Differences: _____

Reasons for Similarities: _____

Comparison: 16th- and 19th-Century Imperialism

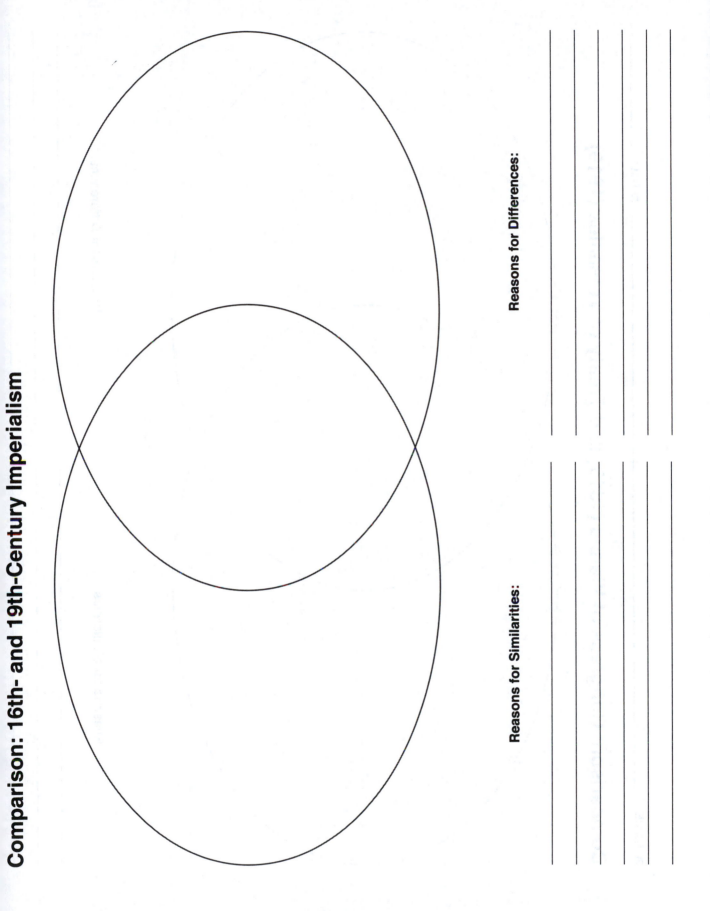

Reasons for Differences:

Reasons for Similarities:

Comparison: Congress of Vienna (1815) and Treaty of Versailles (1919)

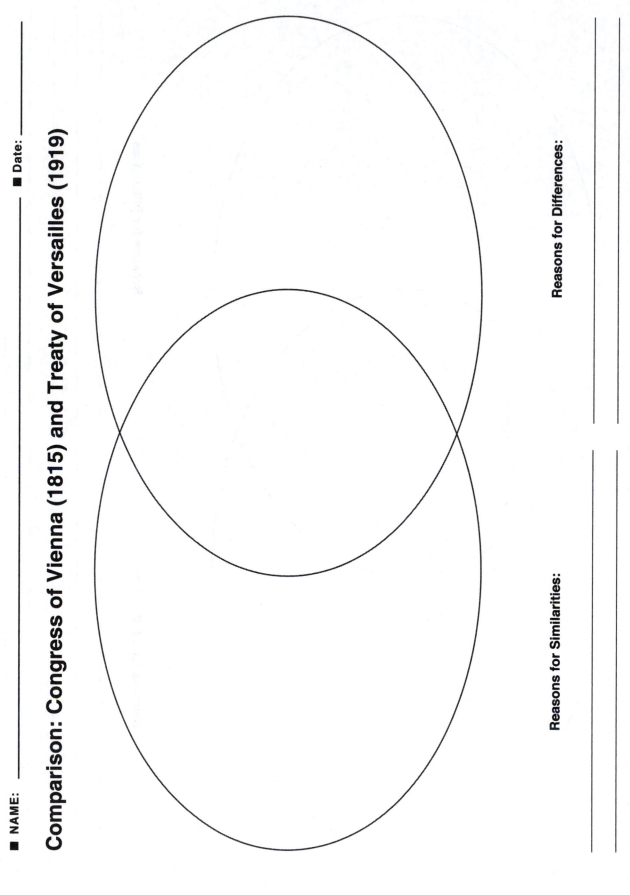

Reasons for Differences:

Reasons for Similarities:

Comparison: Romanticism and Realism

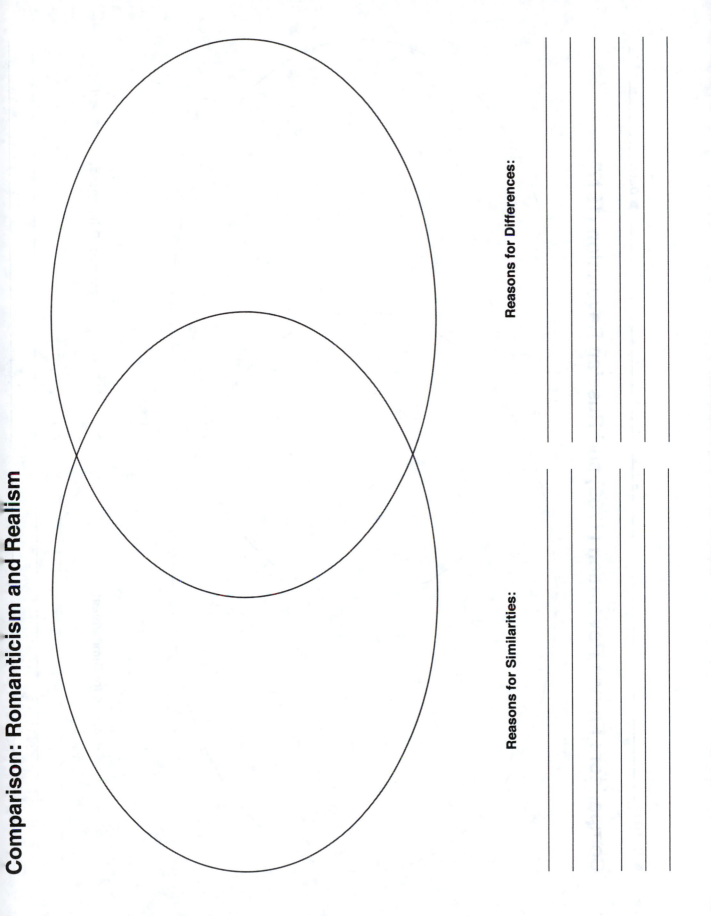

Reasons for Differences:

Reasons for Similarities:

Comparison: French Revolution (1789) and Russian Revolution (1917)

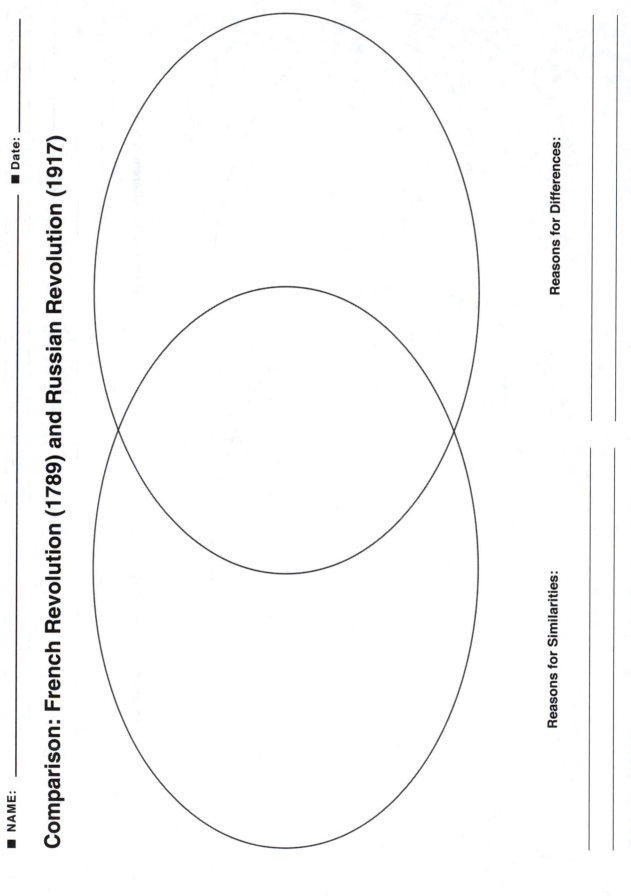

Reasons for Differences:

_____

_____

_____

_____

Reasons for Similarities:

_____

_____

_____

Comparison: Absolutism and Totalitarianism

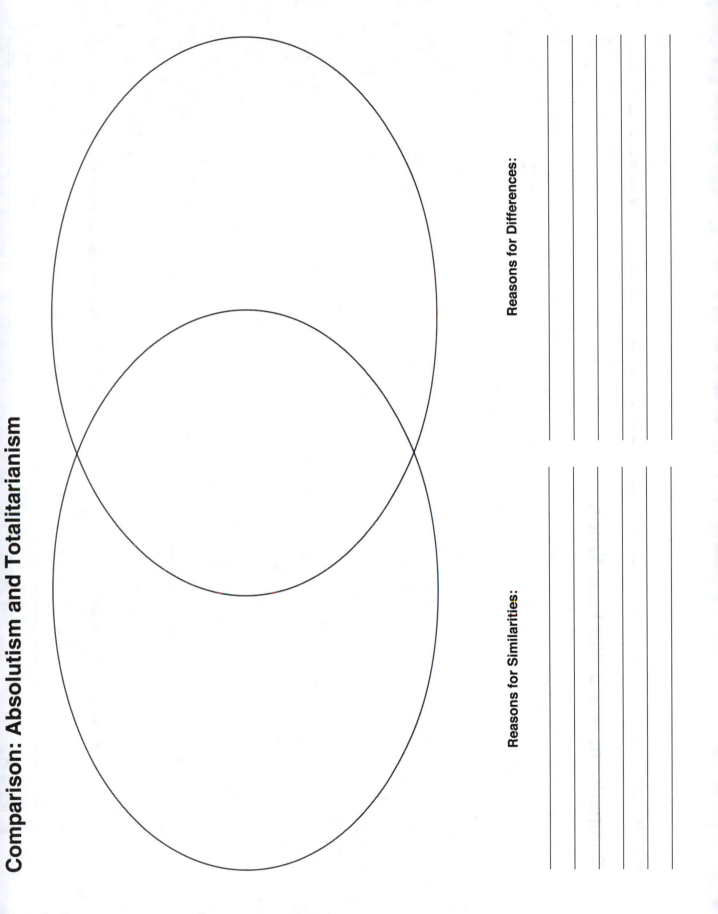

Reasons for Differences:

Reasons for Similarities:

Comparison: World War I and World War II

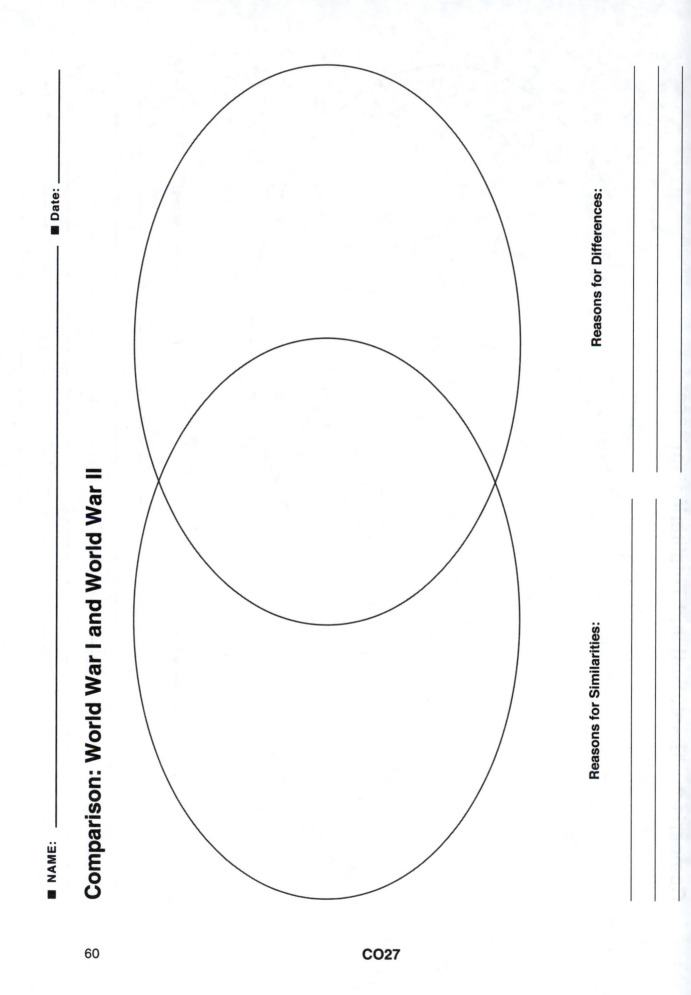

Reasons for Differences:

Reasons for Similarities:

CO27

Comparison: Hitler Youth and French Youth (1968)

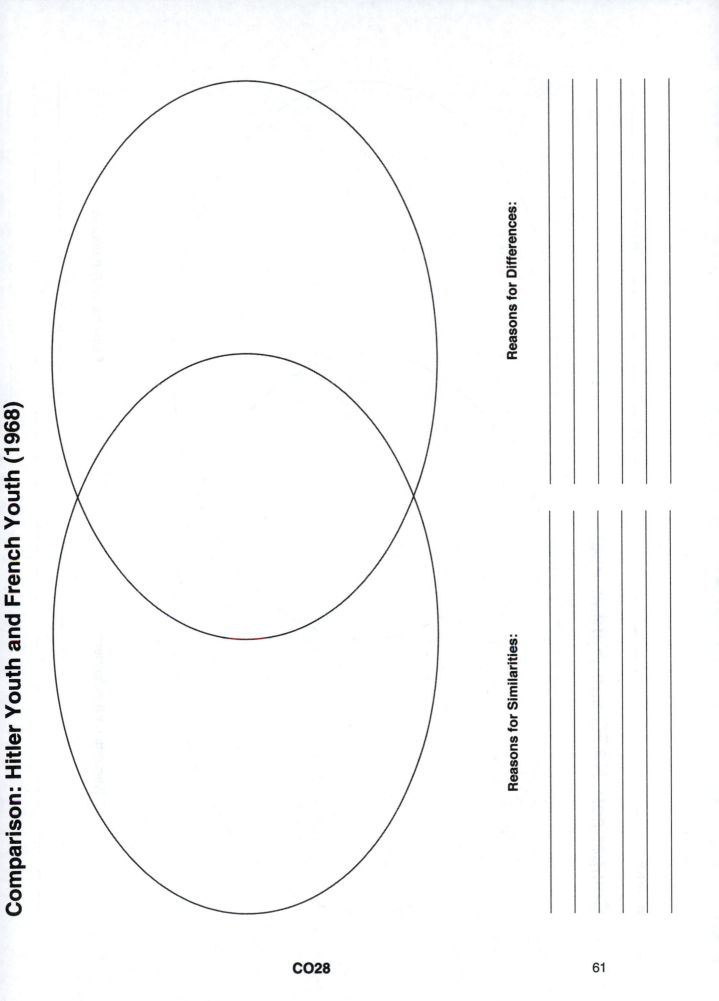

Reasons for Differences:

Reasons for Similarities:

Comparison: NATO and Warsaw Pact

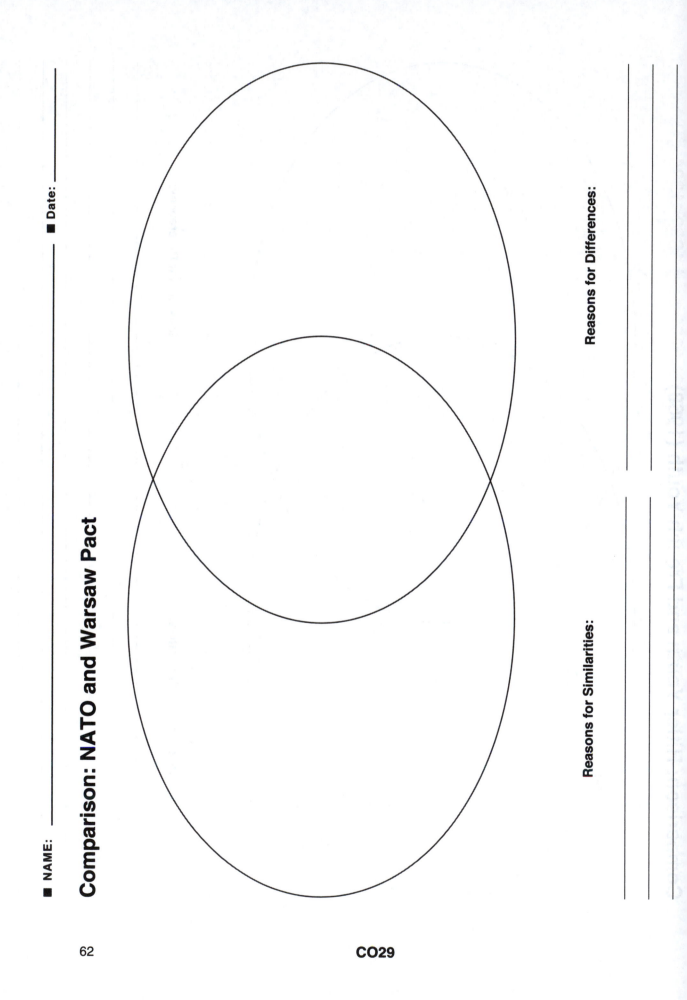

Reasons for Differences:

_____

_____

_____

Reasons for Similarities:

_____

_____

_____

CO29

Comparison: Eastern European Reforms Circa 1953–1968 and 1989–1991

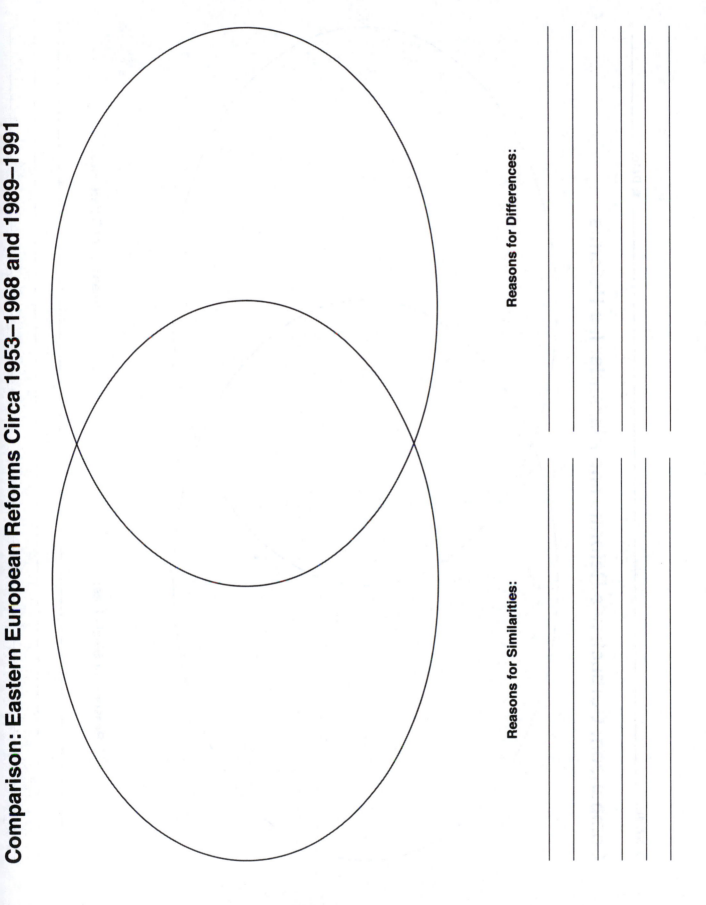

Reasons for Differences:

Reasons for Similarities:

Comparison: Gorbachev's Reforms and Alexander II's Reforms

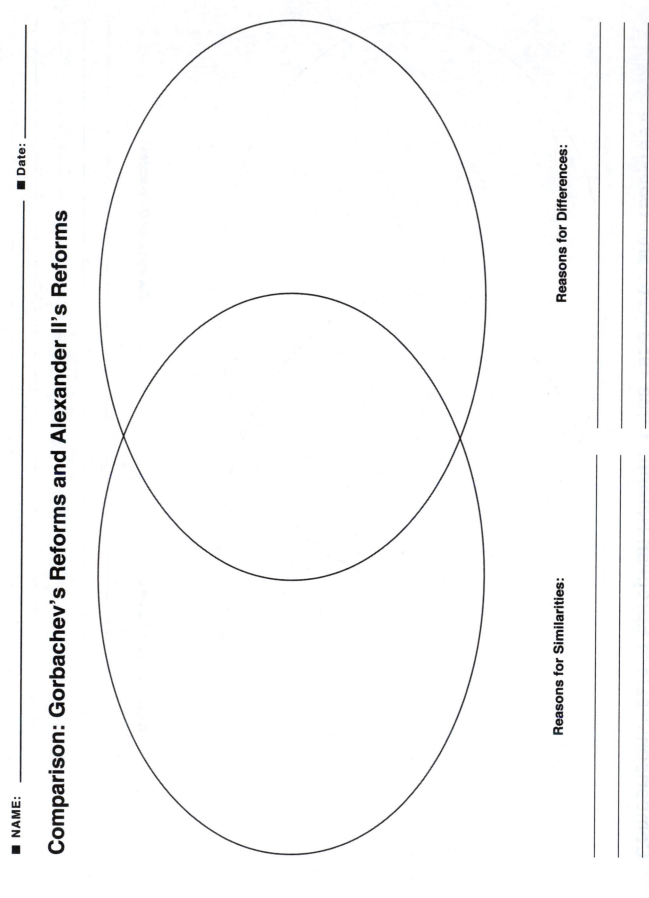

Reasons for Differences:

_____

_____

Reasons for Similarities:

_____

_____

64 **CO31**

Student Instructions: Defining the Period

When we are asked to define a historical period, we are asked to determine specific start and stop dates of events for the period under investigation. Many historical periods do not have clearly defined beginnings and endings; therefore, the task of defining the period is an important one and leads to much debate within historical scholarship.

The purpose of these Defining the Period activities is to investigate when important periods in history begin and end. Each worksheet has a broad historical period about which you are asked to determine when that period begins and ends. In other words, is there some specific historical event or date that you believe defines the beginning and ending of the period under investigation? In addition to determining the beginning and end dates, you will also be asked to provide specific details that help define and contradict the historical period.

Defining the Period: Middle Ages (Example)

Start Date / Event: <u>500 CE</u>
Why?
After the fall of Rome, Western Europe entered into what would be defined as the classical period. The structure of the centralized empire would be left to the rule of regional kingdoms.

End Date / Event: <u>1500 CE</u>
Why?
There is some debate among historians here. Some end it as early as 1000 CE, while others take it to the Enlightenment. Due to the political, social, and economic changes that took place during the high Renaissance, 1500 CE is a popular date.

DEFINING CHARACTERISTICS	CONTRADICTORY CHARACTERISTICS
• Dark Ages • Feudal • Represents a narrow period in European history • Constant war and conflict • Defined by famine and disease • Driven by the church • Fragmented into decentralized regional kingdoms	• It spans 500–1500 CE, which means the Renaissance was part of the Middle Ages. • Carolingian Empire promoted unity. • Though the Church was in a dominant position, its declining power is unclear. • The Hussites offered adverse views on faith before the Reformation.

DP1

Defining the Period: Middle Ages

Start Date / Event:
Why?

_____

_____

_____

End Date / Event:
Why?

_____

_____

_____

DEFINING CHARACTERISTICS	CONTRADICTORY CHARACTERISTICS

Defining the Period: Renaissance

Start Date / Event:
Why?

_____

_____

_____

End Date / Event:
Why?

_____

_____

_____

DEFINING CHARACTERISTICS **CONTRADICTORY CHARACTERISTICS**

Defining the Period: Age of Discovery

Start Date / Event:
Why?

_____
_____
_____

End Date / Event:
Why?

_____
_____
_____

DEFINING CHARACTERISTICS   **CONTRADICTORY CHARACTERISTICS**

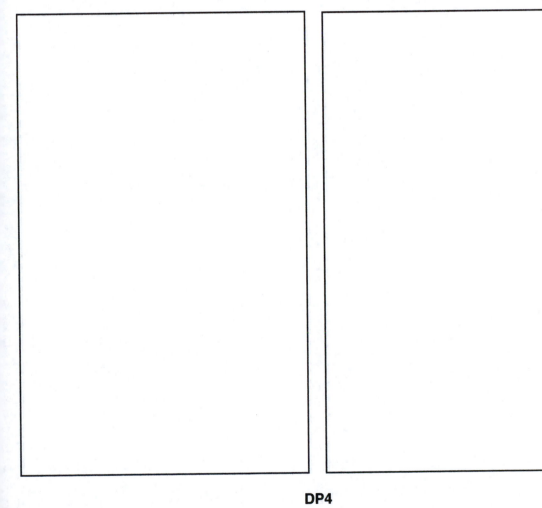

Defining the Period: Elizabethan Era

Start Date / Event:
Why?

_____

_____

_____

End Date / Event:
Why?

_____

_____

_____

DEFINING CHARACTERISTICS	CONTRADICTORY CHARACTERISTICS

Defining the Period: Protestant Reformation

Start Date / Event:
Why?

_____

_____

_____

End Date / Event:
Why?

_____

_____

_____

DEFINING CHARACTERISTICS	**CONTRADICTORY CHARACTERISTICS**

Defining the Period: Classicism

Start Date / Event:
Why?

_____

_____

_____

End Date / Event:
Why?

_____

_____

_____

DEFINING CHARACTERISTICS	CONTRADICTORY CHARACTERISTICS

Defining the Period: Industrious Revolution

Start Date / Event:
Why?

_____
_____
_____

End Date / Event:
Why?

_____
_____
_____

DEFINING CHARACTERISTICS   **CONTRADICTORY CHARACTERISTICS**

Defining the Period: Jacobean Era

Start Date / Event:
Why?

_____
_____
_____

End Date / Event:
Why?

_____
_____
_____

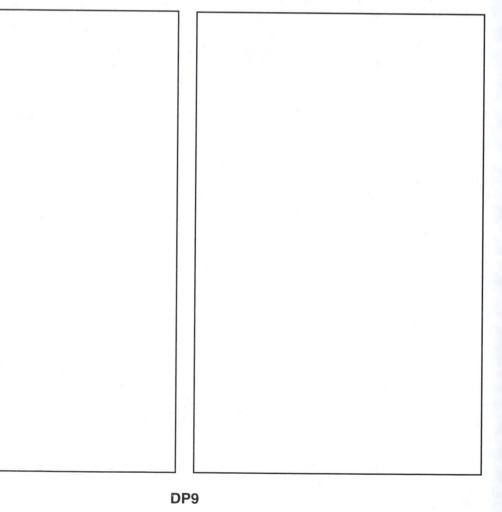

DEFINING CHARACTERISTICS	CONTRADICTORY CHARACTERISTICS

Defining the Period: Age of Absolutism

Start Date / Event:
Why?

_____

_____

_____

End Date / Event:
Why?

_____

_____

_____

DEFINING CHARACTERISTICS	CONTRADICTORY CHARACTERISTICS

Defining the Period: Scientific Revolution

Start Date / Event:
Why?

_____

_____

_____

End Date / Event:
Why?

_____

_____

_____

DEFINING CHARACTERISTICS	CONTRADICTORY CHARACTERISTICS

Defining the Period: Age of Enlightenment

Start Date / Event:
Why?

_____
_____
_____

End Date / Event:
Why?

_____
_____
_____

DEFINING CHARACTERISTICS	CONTRADICTORY CHARACTERISTICS

Defining the Period: French Revolution

Start Date / Event:
Why?

_____

_____

_____

End Date / Event:
Why?

_____

_____

_____

DEFINING CHARACTERISTICS   **CONTRADICTORY CHARACTERISTICS**

Defining the Period: Georgian Era

Start Date / Event:
Why?

_____

_____

_____

End Date / Event:
Why?

_____

_____

_____

DEFINING CHARACTERISTICS	CONTRADICTORY CHARACTERISTICS

Defining the Period: Industrial Revolution

Start Date / Event:
Why?

_____

_____

_____

End Date / Event:
Why?

_____

_____

_____

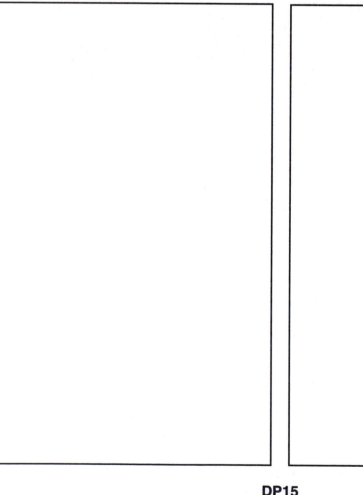

DEFINING CHARACTERISTICS   **CONTRADICTORY CHARACTERISTICS**

Defining the Period: European Imperialism / Colonization

Start Date / Event:
Why?

_____

_____

_____

End Date / Event:
Why?

_____

_____

_____

DEFINING CHARACTERISTICS	CONTRADICTORY CHARACTERISTICS

Defining the Period: Romantic Era

Start Date / Event:
Why?

_____

_____

_____

End Date / Event:
Why?

_____

_____

_____

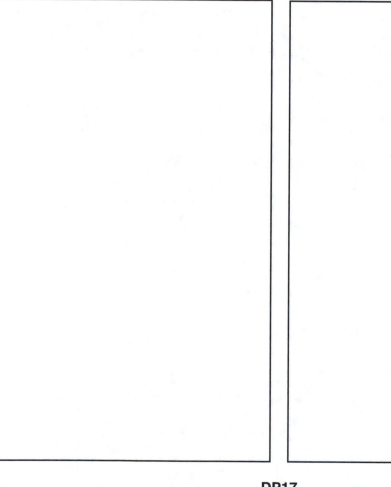

DEFINING CHARACTERISTICS	CONTRADICTORY CHARACTERISTICS

Defining the Period: Napoleonic Era

Start Date / Event:
Why?

_____

_____

_____

End Date / Event:
Why?

_____

_____

_____

DEFINING CHARACTERISTICS	CONTRADICTORY CHARACTERISTICS

Defining the Period: Victorian Era

Start Date / Event:
Why?

_____

_____

_____

End Date / Event:
Why?

_____

_____

_____

DEFINING CHARACTERISTICS	CONTRADICTORY CHARACTERISTICS

Defining the Period: Cold War

Start Date / Event:
Why?

_____
_____
_____

End Date / Event:
Why?

_____
_____
_____

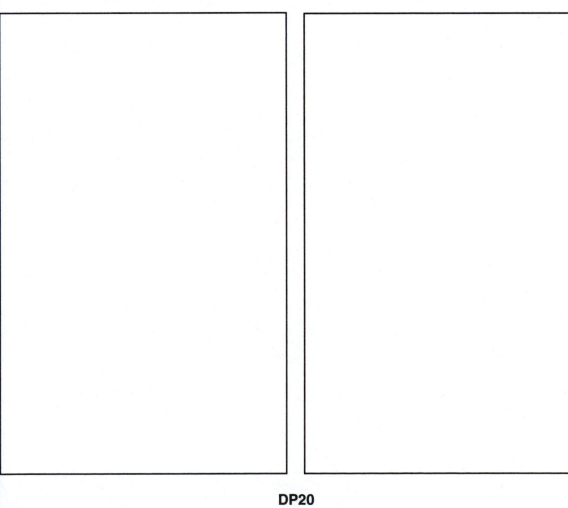

DEFINING CHARACTERISTICS   **CONTRADICTORY CHARACTERISTICS**

Defining the Period: Post–Cold War Europe

Start Date / Event:
Why?

_____
_____
_____

End Date / Event:
Why?

_____
_____
_____

DEFINING CHARACTERISTICS	CONTRADICTORY CHARACTERISTICS

Student Instructions: Contextualization and Synthesis

When we are asked to consider contextualization and synthesis, we are asked to first consider the historical setting of a particular event (i.e., the who, what, when, where, and why) and then to connect that event to another event in history.

The purpose of the Contextualization and Synthesis activities is to explore the different ways in which historians work with context. The first is what we call Broad Context: the big picture. The second is what we call Other Context: the connection of the topic under investigation to another period by looking either backward or forward —"similar in kind, but at a different time."

Contextualization and Synthesis: Donation of Constantine (Example)

Contextualization

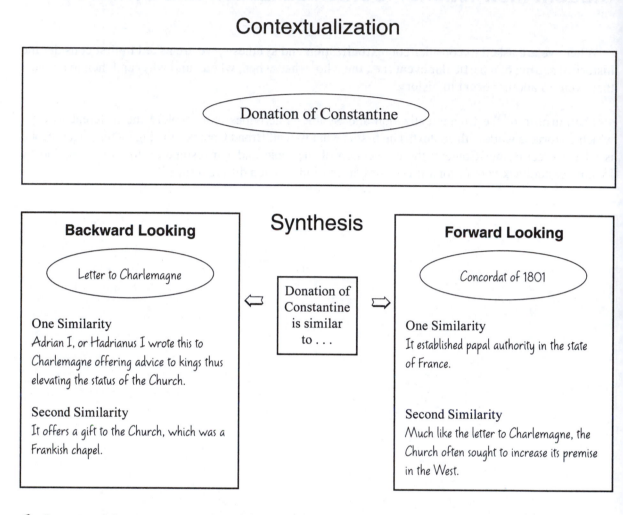

Donation of Constantine

Synthesis

Backward Looking

Letter to Charlemagne

One Similarity
Adrian I, or Hadrianus I wrote this to Charlemagne offering advice to kings thus elevating the status of the Church.

Second Similarity
It offers a gift to the Church, which was a Frankish chapel.

Donation of Constantine is similar to . . .

Forward Looking

Concordat of 1801

One Similarity
It established papal authority in the state of France.

Second Similarity
Much like the letter to Charlemagne, the Church often sought to increase its premise in the West.

The Donation of Constantine was a forged document of the 8th century, giving the pope authority over former Roman lands. By the high Renaissance, Lorenzo Valla, drawing off new critiques and emerging doubts about papal authority, discovered the document was fake. Valla's conclusion about the document further notes the period as one of discovery.

_____

_____

_____

_____

_____

_____

_____

Contextualization and Synthesis: Donation of Constantine

Contextualization

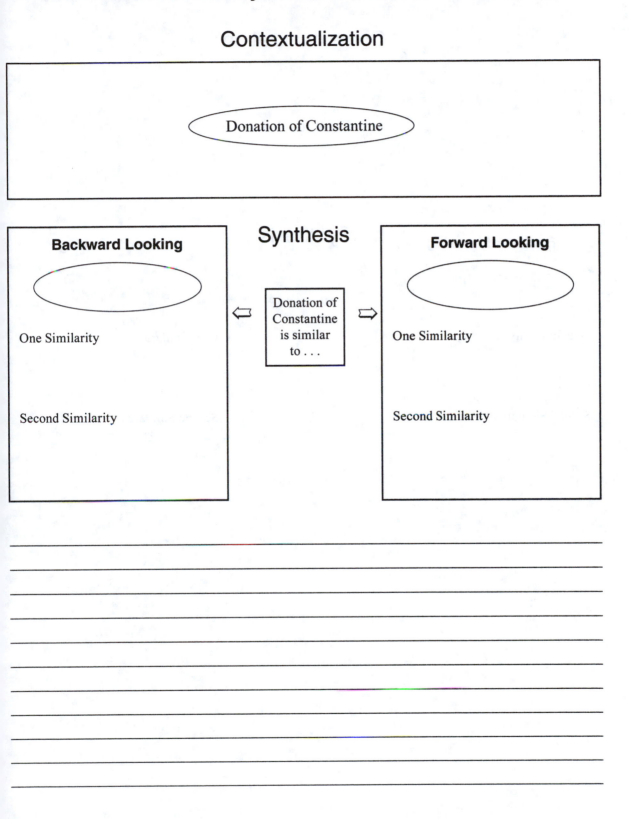

Donation of Constantine

Synthesis

Backward Looking

One Similarity

Second Similarity

Donation of
Constantine
is similar
to . . .

Forward Looking

One Similarity

Second Similarity

Contextualization and Synthesis: War of the Roses

Contextualization

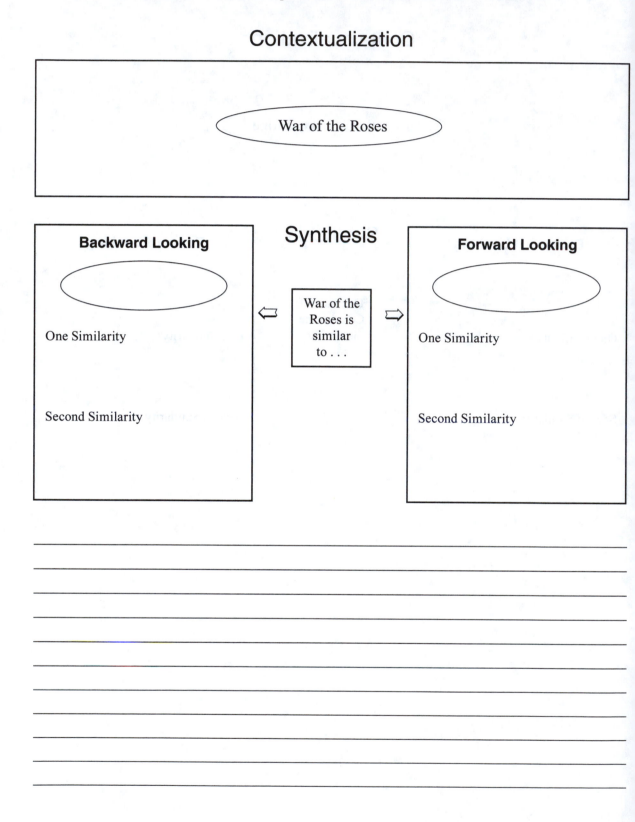

War of the Roses

Synthesis

Backward Looking

One Similarity

Second Similarity

War of the
Roses is
similar
to . . .

Forward Looking

One Similarity

Second Similarity

_____
_____
_____
_____
_____
_____
_____
_____
_____
_____

CS3

Contextualization and Synthesis: New Monarchy

Contextualization

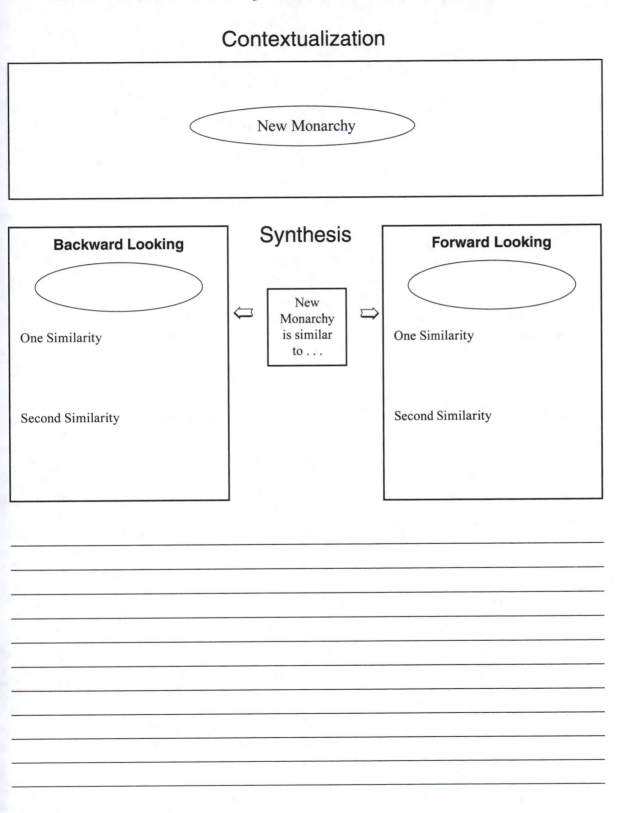

New Monarchy

Synthesis

Backward Looking

One Similarity

Second Similarity

New Monarchy is similar to . . .

Forward Looking

One Similarity

Second Similarity

Contextualization and Synthesis: Spanish Inquisition

Contextualization

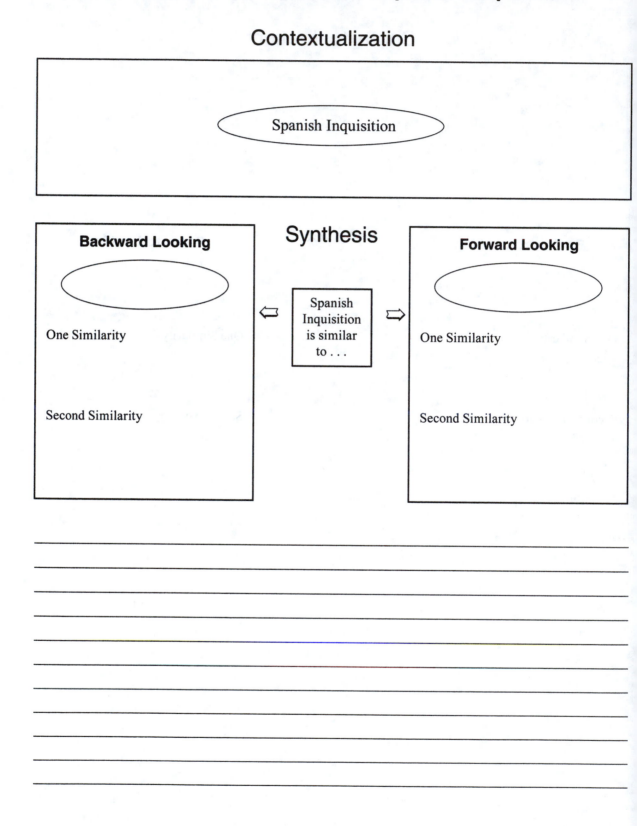

Spanish Inquisition

Synthesis

Backward Looking

One Similarity

Second Similarity

Spanish Inquisition is similar to . . .

Forward Looking

One Similarity

Second Similarity

Contextualization and Synthesis: Price Revolution

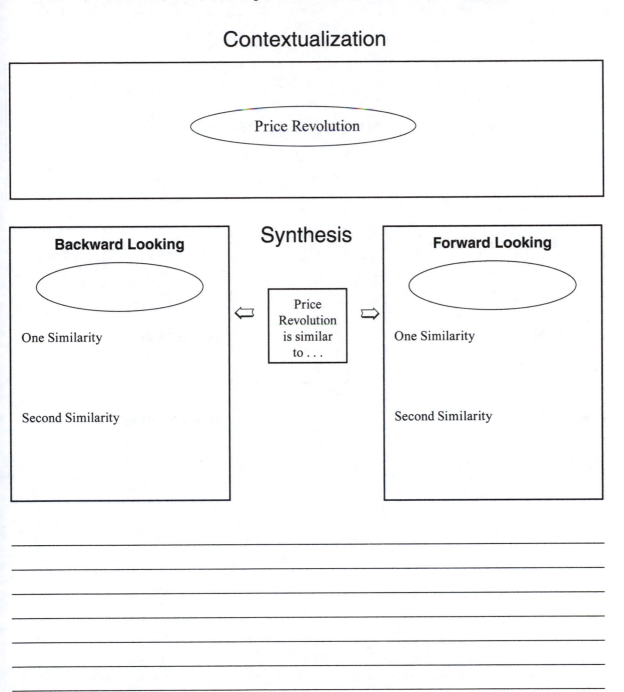

Contextualization

Price Revolution

Synthesis

Backward Looking

One Similarity

Second Similarity

Price Revolution is similar to . . .

Forward Looking

One Similarity

Second Similarity

Contextualization and Synthesis: Act of Supremacy, 1534

Contextualization

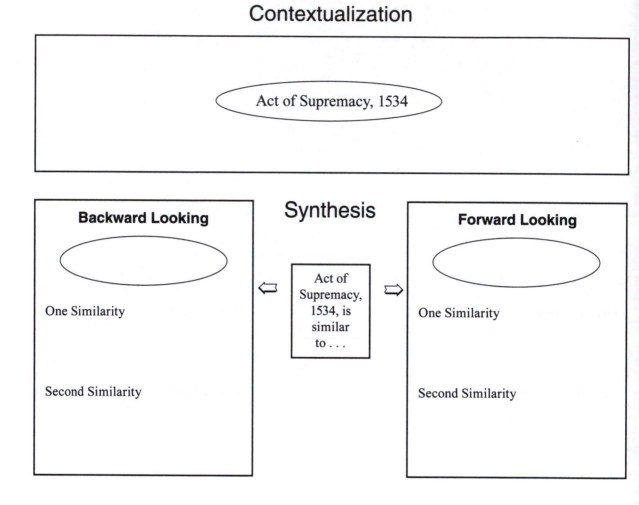

Act of Supremacy, 1534

Synthesis

Backward Looking

One Similarity

Second Similarity

Act of Supremacy, 1534, is similar to . . .

Forward Looking

One Similarity

Second Similarity

_____
_____
_____
_____
_____
_____
_____
_____
_____
_____
_____

CS7

Contextualization and Synthesis: 95 Theses

Contextualization

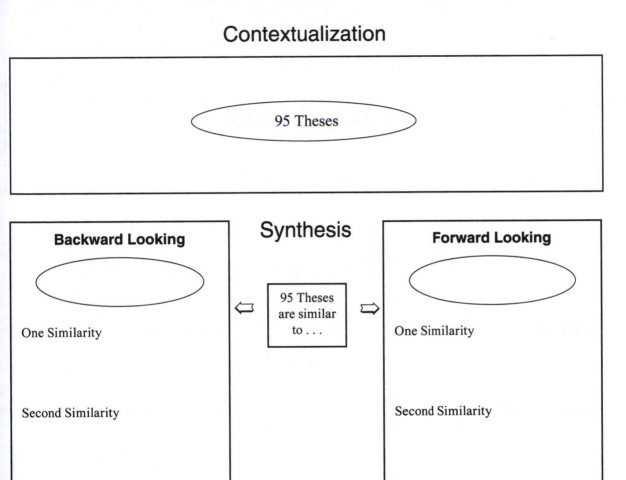

Contextualization and Synthesis: *Cuius Regio, Eius Religio*

Contextualization

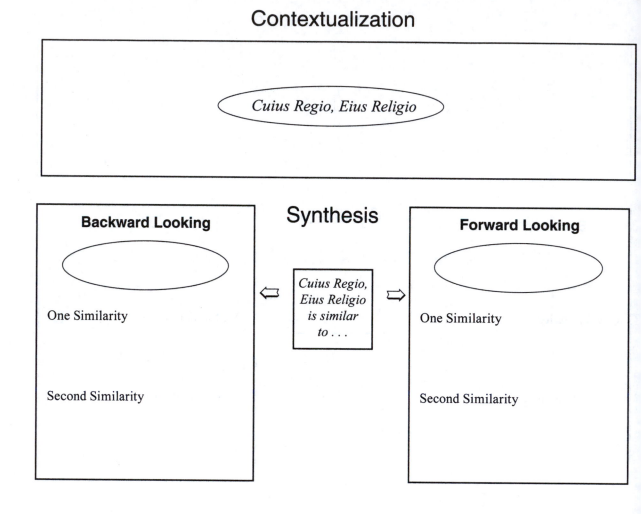

Cuius Regio, Eius Religio

Synthesis

Backward Looking

One Similarity

Second Similarity

Cuius Regio, Eius Religio is similar to . . .

Forward Looking

One Similarity

Second Similarity

Contextualization and Synthesis: English Restoration

Contextualization

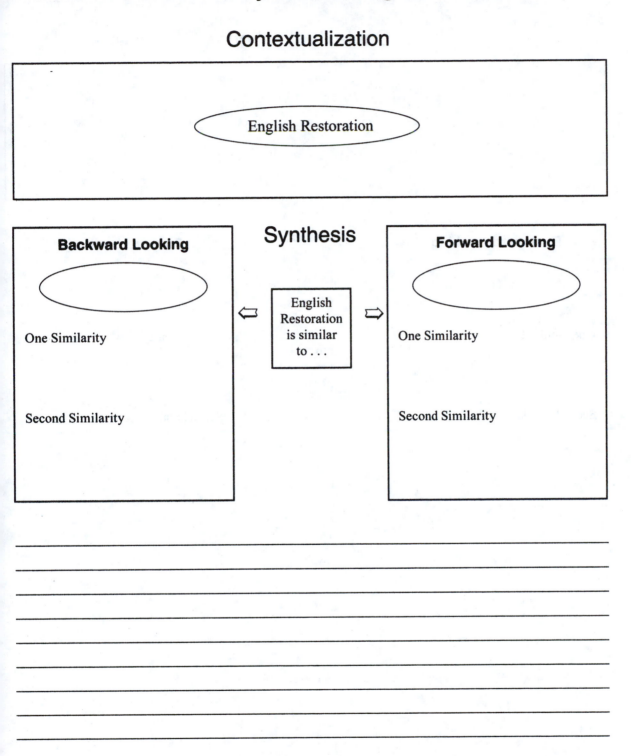

English Restoration

Synthesis

Backward Looking

One Similarity

Second Similarity

English Restoration is similar to . . .

Forward Looking

One Similarity

Second Similarity

_____

_____

_____

_____

_____

_____

_____

_____

_____

_____

_____

Contextualization and Synthesis: Glorious Revolution

Contextualization

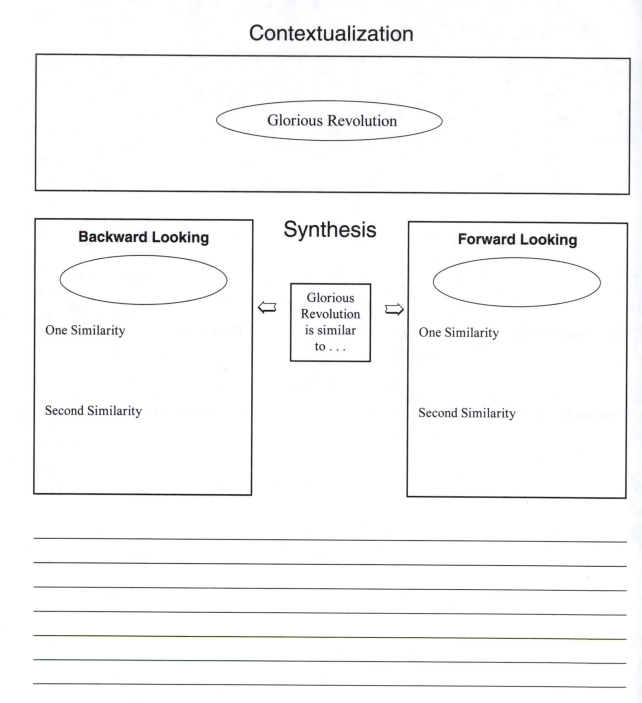

Glorious Revolution

Synthesis

Backward Looking

One Similarity

Second Similarity

Glorious Revolution is similar to . . .

Forward Looking

One Similarity

Second Similarity

_____
_____
_____
_____
_____
_____
_____
_____
_____
_____
_____

CS11

Contextualization and Synthesis: Pugachev's Rebellion

Contextualization

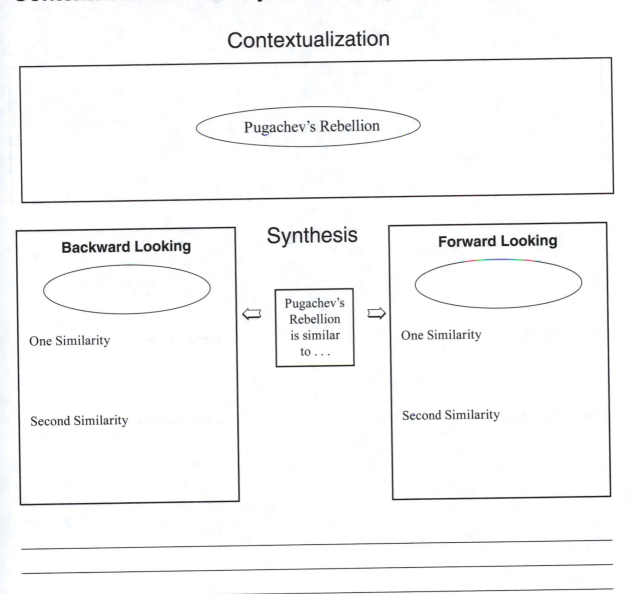

Pugachev's Rebellion

Synthesis

Backward Looking

One Similarity

Second Similarity

Pugachev's Rebellion is similar to . . .

Forward Looking

One Similarity

Second Similarity

Contextualization and Synthesis: Enlightened Despots

Contextualization

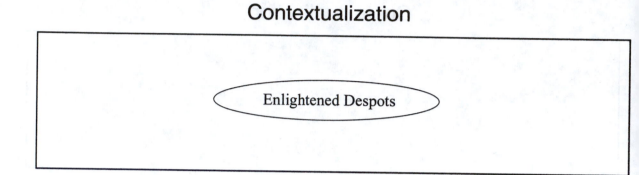

Enlightened Despots

Synthesis

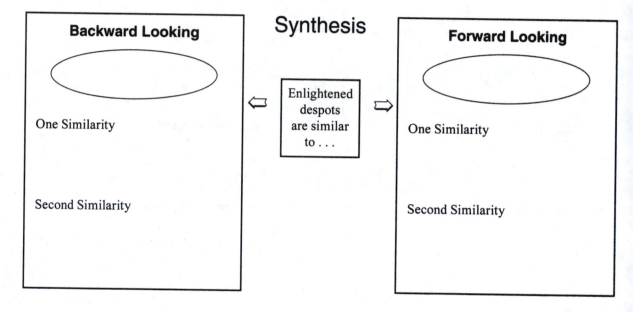

Backward Looking

One Similarity

Second Similarity

Enlightened despots are similar to . . .

Forward Looking

One Similarity

Second Similarity

CS13

Contextualization and Synthesis: Ancien Regime

Contextualization

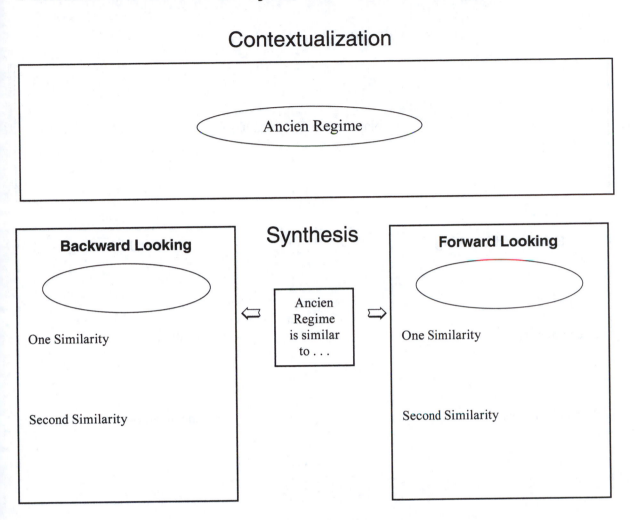

Backward Looking		Forward Looking

Synthesis

One Similarity

Second Similarity

Ancien Regime is similar to . . .

One Similarity

Second Similarity

Contextualization and Synthesis: Napoleon's Concordat

Contextualization

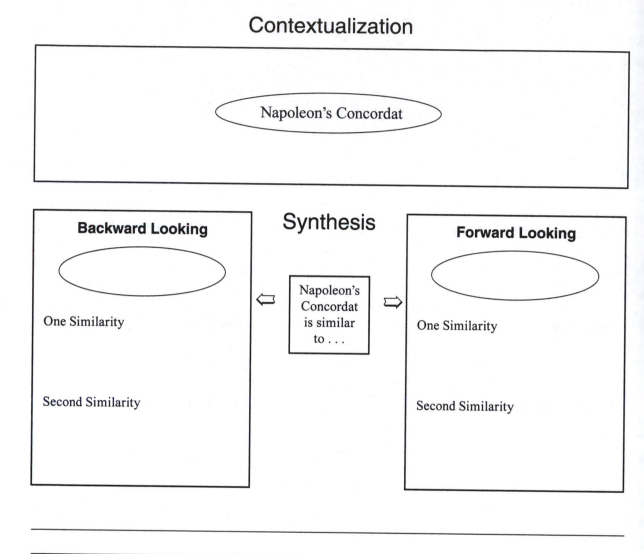

Napoleon's Concordat

Synthesis

Backward Looking

One Similarity

Second Similarity

Napoleon's Concordat is similar to . . .

Forward Looking

One Similarity

Second Similarity

Contextualization and Synthesis: Congress System

Contextualization

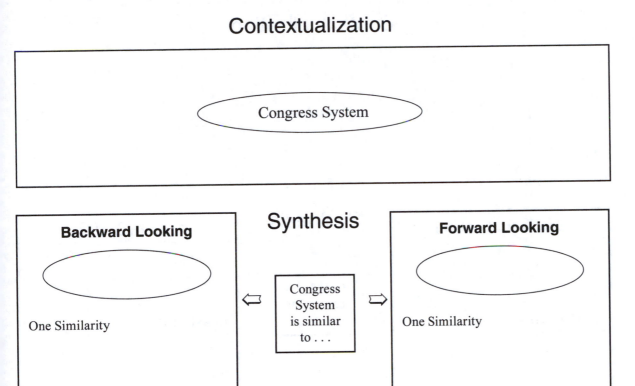

Congress System

Synthesis

Backward Looking

One Similarity

Second Similarity

Congress
System
is similar
to . . .

Forward Looking

One Similarity

Second Similarity

_____

_____

_____

_____

_____

_____

_____

_____

_____

_____

_____

_____

Contextualization and Synthesis: Corn Laws

Contextualization

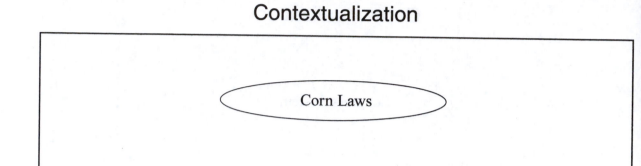

Synthesis

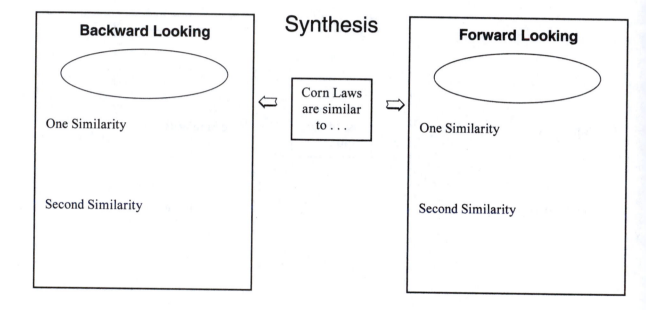

_____
_____
_____
_____
_____
_____
_____
_____
_____
_____
_____
_____

Contextualization and Synthesis: Irish Potato Famine, 1826

Contextualization

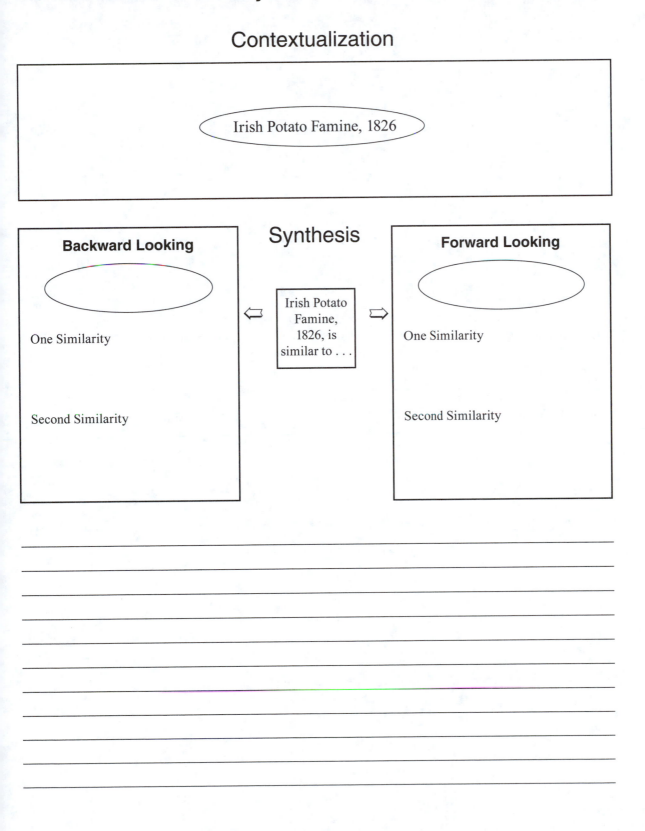

(Irish Potato Famine, 1826)

Synthesis

Backward Looking

⇐ | Irish Potato Famine, 1826, is similar to . . . | ⇒

One Similarity

Second Similarity

Forward Looking

One Similarity

Second Similarity

Contextualization and Synthesis: *Communist Manifesto*

Contextualization

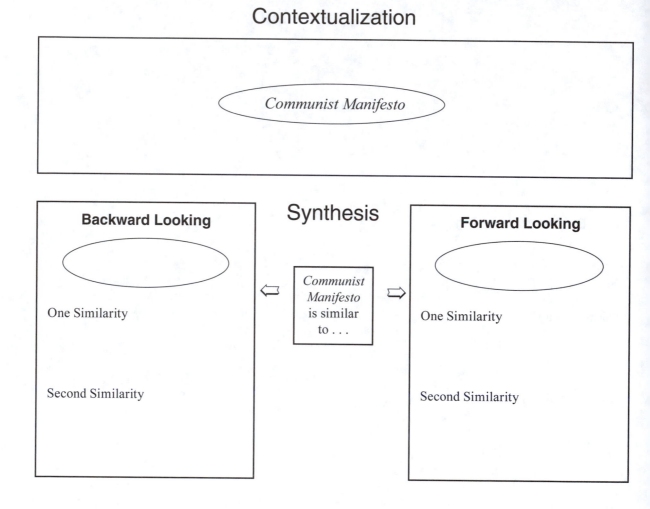

106   **CS19**

Contextualization and Synthesis: Frankfurt Parliament

Contextualization

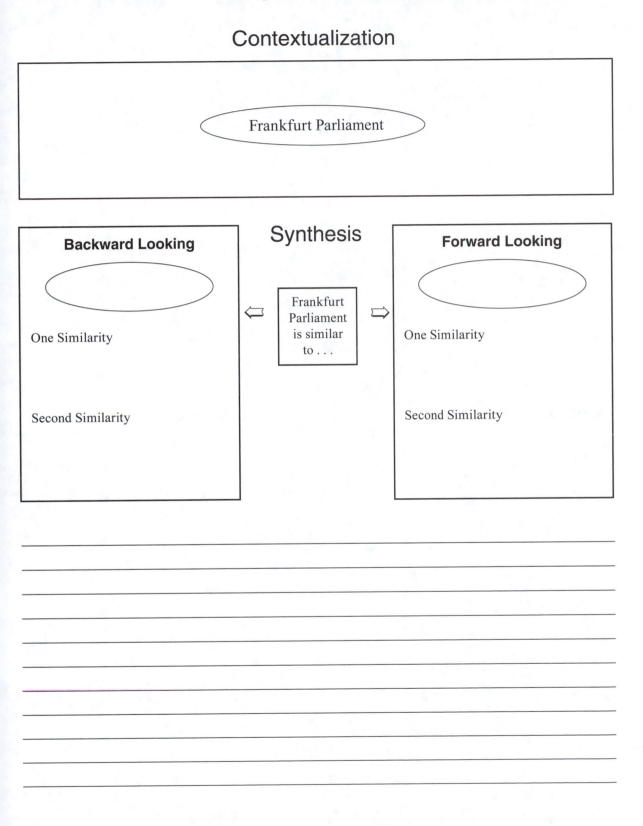

Frankfurt Parliament

Synthesis

Backward Looking

One Similarity

Second Similarity

Frankfurt
Parliament
is similar
to . . .

Forward Looking

One Similarity

Second Similarity

Contextualization and Synthesis: Realpolitik

Contextualization

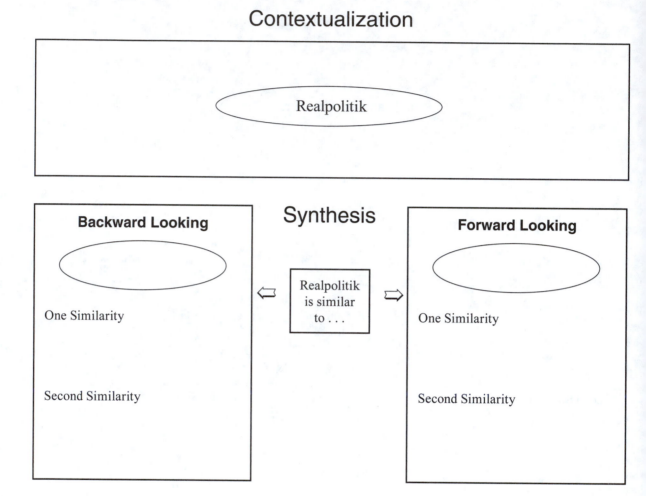

Synthesis

Backward Looking

One Similarity

Second Similarity

Realpolitik
is similar
to . . .

Forward Looking

One Similarity

Second Similarity

Contextualization and Synthesis: Alfred Dreyfus Affair

Contextualization

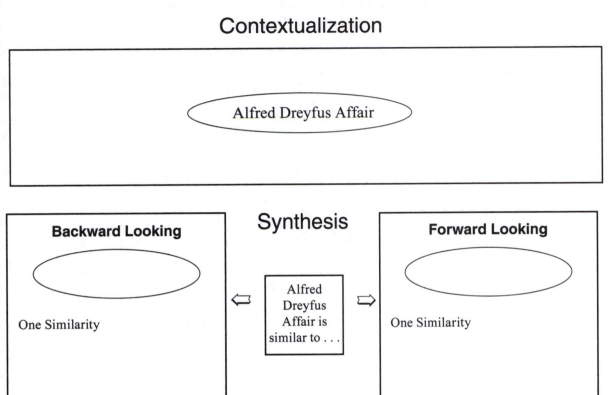

Alfred Dreyfus Affair

Synthesis

Backward Looking

One Similarity

Second Similarity

Alfred Dreyfus Affair is similar to . . .

Forward Looking

One Similarity

Second Similarity

_____
_____
_____
_____
_____
_____
_____
_____
_____
_____
_____
_____

Contextualization and Synthesis: Congress of Berlin, 1884

Contextualization

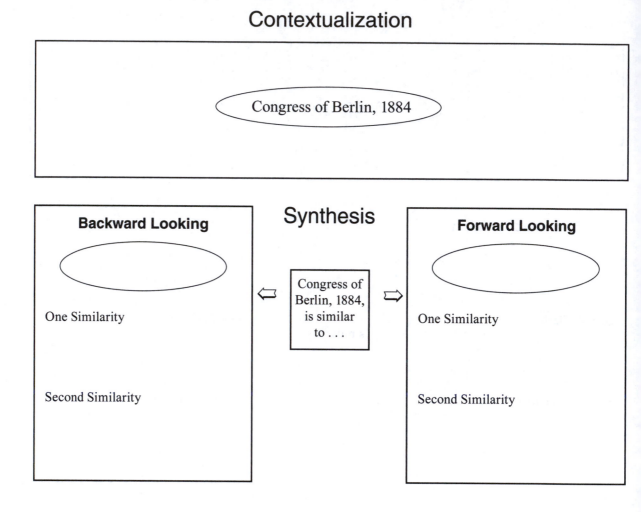

Synthesis

Backward Looking

One Similarity

Second Similarity

Congress of Berlin, 1884, is similar to . . .

Forward Looking

One Similarity

Second Similarity

Contextualization and Synthesis: Five-Year Plans

Contextualization

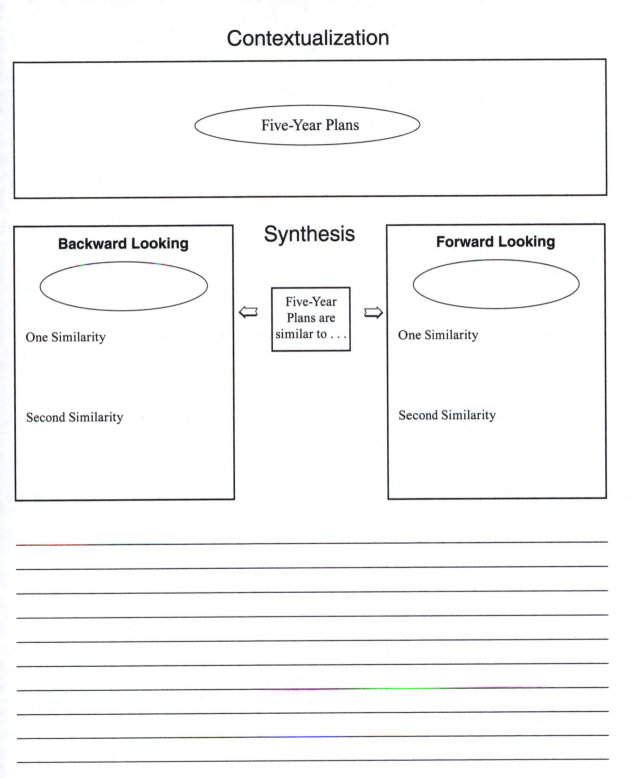

One Similarity

Second Similarity

One Similarity

Second Similarity

_____

_____

_____

_____

_____

_____

_____

_____

_____

_____

_____

_____

Contextualization and Synthesis: Article 231

Contextualization

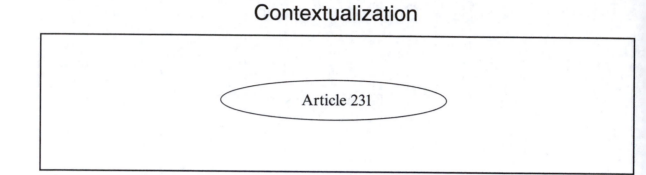

Synthesis

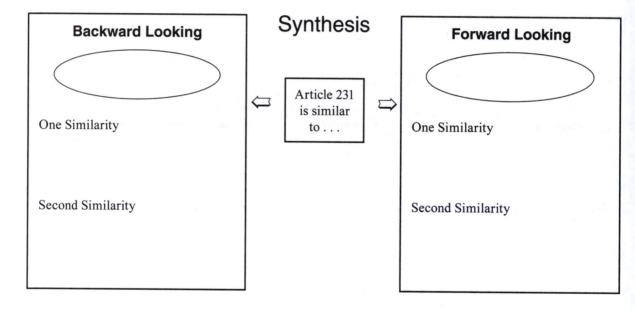

_____
_____
_____
_____
_____
_____
_____
_____
_____
_____
_____
_____

CS25

Contextualization and Synthesis: Balfour Declaration

Contextualization

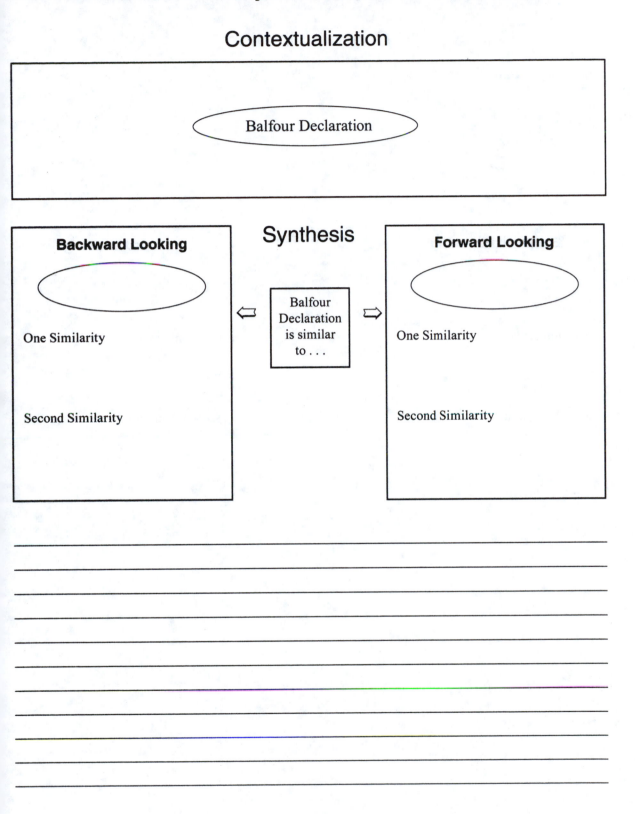

Balfour Declaration

Synthesis

Backward Looking

One Similarity

Second Similarity

Balfour
Declaration
is similar
to . . .

Forward Looking

One Similarity

Second Similarity

Contextualization and Synthesis: Final Solution

Contextualization

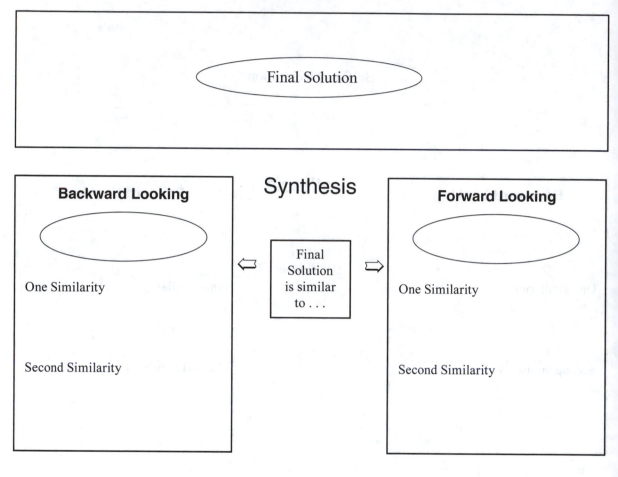

Synthesis

Backward Looking

One Similarity

Second Similarity

Final Solution is similar to . . .

Forward Looking

One Similarity

Second Similarity

_____
_____
_____
_____
_____
_____
_____
_____
_____
_____
_____
_____

Contextualization and Synthesis: Potsdam Settlement

Contextualization

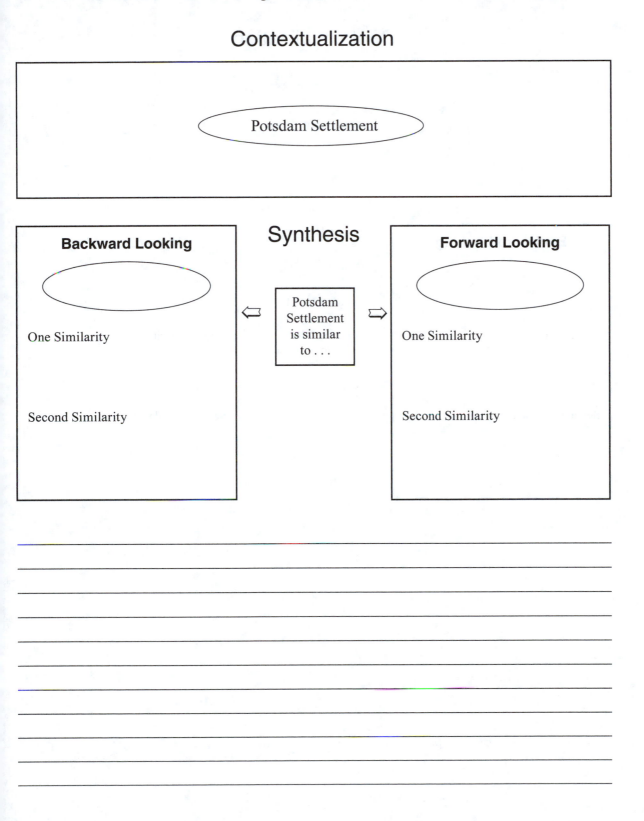

Potsdam Settlement

Synthesis

Backward Looking

One Similarity

Second Similarity

Potsdam
Settlement
is similar
to . . .

Forward Looking

One Similarity

Second Similarity

Contextualization and Synthesis: Maastricht Treaty

Contextualization

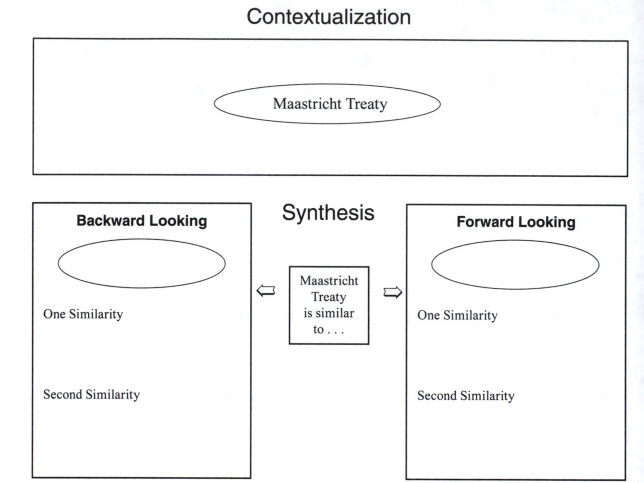

Maastricht Treaty

Synthesis

Backward Looking

One Similarity

Second Similarity

Maastricht Treaty is similar to . . .

Forward Looking

One Similarity

Second Similarity

_____
_____
_____
_____
_____
_____
_____
_____
_____
_____
_____
_____

Contextualization and Synthesis: Brezhnev Doctrine

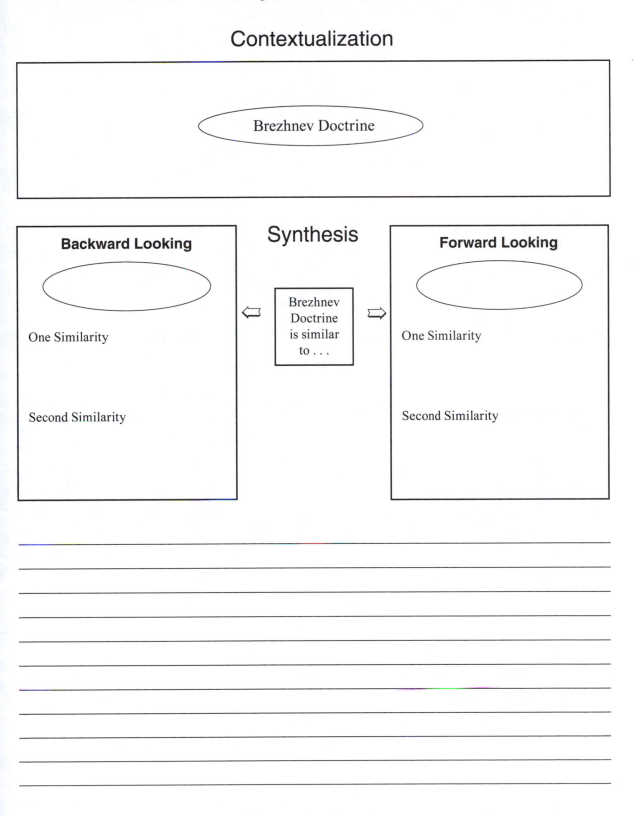

Contextualization

Brezhnev Doctrine

Synthesis

Backward Looking

One Similarity

Second Similarity

Brezhnev Doctrine is similar to . . .

Forward Looking

One Similarity

Second Similarity

Contextualization and Synthesis: Glasnost and Perestroika

Contextualization

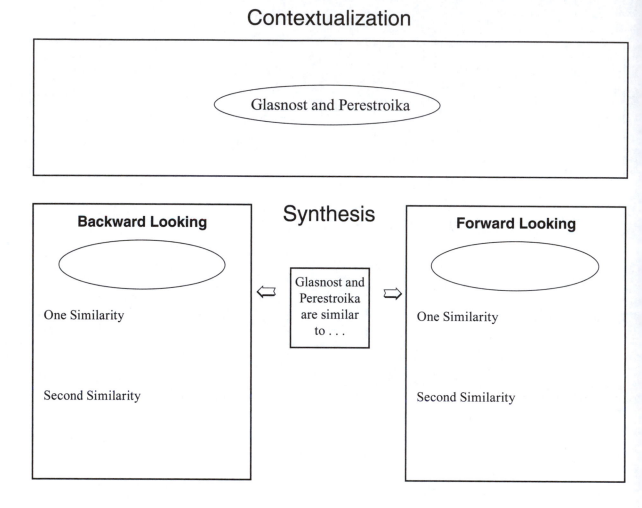

Glasnost and Perestroika

Synthesis

Backward Looking

One Similarity

Second Similarity

Glasnost and Perestroika are similar to . . .

Forward Looking

One Similarity

Second Similarity

Student Instructions: Turning Point

When we are asked to determine a turning point, we are asked to determine how a single event brought about significant change in history. This is different from looking at continuity and change over time, which normally requires us to consider multiple events and gives us a defined time period. Determining a turning point involves focusing on a single event and determining to what extent that event served as a major turning point in history.

The purpose of these Turning Point activities is to explain the historical context of each of the three events and then determine which one of the events constitutes a turning point in history. These worksheets prompt us to discuss what history was like before and after a particular event, helping us to confirm whether the event is, in fact, a turning point.

Turning Point: Medieval World (Example)

Give specific historical details about the three events listed below (e.g., who, what, when, where, why).

Kievan Rus' taken by the Mongols:

The Kievan Rus' adopted Christianity via the economic trade exchange with the Byzantine empire following the classical period. They would slowly allow cultural assimilation of the Mongol people, bringing an end to the Yuan Dynasty and the birth of Slavic Russians.

Babylonian Captivity:

The king of France announced his pope selection and placed him in Avignon. This promoted what is known as the Great Schism, roughly in the 14th century. This religious and political division transpired 30 years.

Spread of the Black Death:

Nomads, merchants, and travelers who came into contact with migrants from Asia transfered the disease to the West. It would hit Italy first, before spreading throughout Europe.

Select one of the above events you believe to be a turning point in European history, then describe what it was like before and after that event.

Europe prior to the event:

Before the plague hit Europe, states were decentralized while towns were growing. Commerce after 1000 picked up. Feudalism remained, though a growing middle/merchant class had emerged.

Europe after the event:

After 1350 CE, Europe slowly entered the low Renaissance. Feudalism had started to decline, and peasants found greater freedom. The church struggled to maintain the level of power it once held.

Turning Point: Medieval World

Give specific historical details about the three events listed below (e.g., who, what, when, where, why).

Kievan Rus' taken by the Mongols:

_____
_____
_____
_____

Babylonian Captivity:

_____
_____
_____
_____

Spread of the Black Death:

_____
_____
_____
_____

Select one of the above events you believe to be a turning point in European history, then describe what it was like before and after that event.

Europe prior to the event:

_____
_____
_____
_____

Europe after the event:

_____
_____
_____
_____

Turning Point: Rebirth and Unrest

Give specific historical details about the three events listed below (e.g., who, what, when, where, why).

Great Schism begins:

_____
_____
_____
_____

English Peasant Revolt:

_____
_____
_____
_____

Constantinople falls to the Ottoman Turks:

_____
_____
_____
_____

Select one of the above events you believe to be a turning point in European history, then describe what it was like before and after that event.

Europe prior to the event:

_____
_____
_____
_____

Europe after the event:

_____
_____
_____
_____

Turning Point: Innovation and Exploration

Give specific historical details about the three events listed below (e.g., who, what, when, where, why).

Gutenberg Printing Press:

_____

_____

_____

_____

Voyage of Columbus:

_____

_____

_____

_____

Publication of *The Prince* by Machiavelli:

_____

_____

_____

_____

Select one of the above events you believe to be a turning point in European history, then describe what it was like before and after that event.

Europe prior to the event:

_____

_____

_____

_____

Europe after the event:

_____

_____

_____

_____

Turning Point: Dissent and Division

Give specific historical details about the three events listed below (e.g., who, what, when, where, why).

Luther posts 95 Theses:

_____

_____

_____

_____

Henry VIII establishes Church of England:

_____

_____

_____

_____

Council of Trent convened:

_____

_____

_____

_____

Select one of the above events you believe to be a turning point in European history, then describe what it was like before and after that event.

Europe prior to the event:

_____

_____

_____

_____

Europe after the event:

_____

_____

_____

_____

Turning Point: Atlantic World

Give specific historical details about the three events listed below (e.g., who, what, when, where, why).

Peace of Augsburg:

_____

_____

_____

_____

Founding of Jamestown:

_____

_____

_____

_____

Dutch West India Company founded:

_____

_____

_____

_____

Select one of the above events you believe to be a turning point in European history, then describe what it was like before and after that event.

Europe prior to the event:

_____

_____

_____

_____

Europe after the event:

_____

_____

_____

_____

Turning Point: Monarchies and Absolutism

Give specific historical details about the three events listed below (e.g., who, what, when, where, why).

Reign of Louis XIV:

_____
_____
_____
_____

Revocation of the Edict of Nantes:

_____
_____
_____
_____

War of Spanish Succession:

_____
_____
_____
_____

Select one of the above events you believe to be a turning point in European history, then describe what it was like before and after that event.

Europe prior to the event:

_____
_____
_____
_____

Europe after the event:

_____
_____
_____
_____

Turning Point: New Science

Give specific historical details about the three events listed below (e.g., who, what, when, where, why).

Copernicus publishes *On the Revolutions*:

_____
_____
_____
_____

Galileo Trial:

_____
_____
_____
_____

Royal Society of London founded:

_____
_____
_____
_____

Select one of the above events you believe to be a turning point in European history, then describe what it was like before and after that event.

Europe prior to the event:

_____
_____
_____

Europe after the event:

_____
_____
_____
_____

Turning Point: Enlightenment

Give specific historical details about the three events listed below (e.g., who, what, when, where, why).

Locke publishes *On Human Understanding*:

_____
_____
_____
_____

American Revolution:

_____
_____
_____
_____

Smith publishes *Wealth of Nations*:

_____
_____
_____
_____

Select one of the above events you believe to be a turning point in European history, then describe what it was like before and after that event.

Europe prior to the event:

_____
_____
_____
_____

Europe after the event:

_____
_____
_____
_____

Turning Point: French Revolution

Give specific historical details about the three events listed below (e.g., who, what, when, where, why).

Estates General meets:

_____

_____

_____

_____

Fall of the Bastille:

_____

_____

_____

_____

Napoleon crowned Emperor:

_____

_____

_____

_____

Select one of the above events you believe to be a turning point in European history, then describe what it was like before and after that event.

Europe prior to the event:

_____

_____

_____

_____

Europe after the event:

_____

_____

_____

_____

Turning Point: Industrial Revolution

Give specific historical details about the three events listed below (e.g., who, what, when, where, why).

First Railroad in Britain:

_____
_____
_____
_____

Irish Potato Famine:

_____
_____
_____
_____

Russian Tsar emancipates the Serfs:

_____
_____
_____
_____

Select one of the above events you believe to be a turning point in European history, then describe what it was like before and after that event.

Europe prior to the event:

_____
_____
_____
_____

Europe after the event:

_____
_____
_____
_____

Turning Point: Age of Ideologies

Give specific historical details about the three events listed below (e.g., who, what, when, where, why).

Congress of Vienna:

_____

_____

_____

_____

British Reform Bill:

_____

_____

_____

_____

Marx publishes *Communist Manifesto*:

_____

_____

_____

_____

Select one of the above events you believe to be a turning point in European history, then describe what it was like before and after that event.

Europe prior to the event:

_____

_____

_____

Europe after the event:

_____

_____

_____

_____

Turning Point: Revolutions and Nation Building

Give specific historical details about the three events listed below (e.g., who, what, when, where, why).

Unification of Germany:

_____
_____
_____
_____

Revolutions of 1848:

_____
_____
_____
_____

Crimean War:

_____
_____
_____
_____

Select one of the above events you believe to be a turning point in European history, then describe what it was like before and after that event.

Europe prior to the event:

_____
_____
_____

Europe after the event:

_____
_____
_____
_____

Turning Point: Imperialism and Colonialism

Give specific historical details about the three events listed below (e.g., who, what, when, where, why).

British Expansion to India:

_____
_____
_____
_____

France into Vietnam:

_____
_____
_____
_____

Spanish-American War:

_____
_____
_____
_____

Select one of the above events you believe to be a turning point in European history, then describe what it was like before and after that event.

Europe prior to the event:

_____
_____
_____
_____

Europe after the event:

_____
_____
_____
_____

Turning Point: Modern Industry and Mass Politics

Give specific historical details about the three events listed below (e.g., who, what, when, where, why).

Production of Steel Alloys revolutionized:

_____
_____
_____
_____

Electrification of the City:

_____
_____
_____
_____

British Labour Party founded:

_____
_____
_____
_____

Select one of the above events you believe to be a turning point in European history, then describe what it was like before and after that event.

Europe prior to the event:

_____
_____
_____
_____

Europe after the event:

_____
_____
_____
_____

Turning Point: WWI

Give specific historical details about the three events listed below (e.g., who, what, when, where, why).

Dual Alliance:

_____
_____
_____
_____

United States enters the War:

_____
_____
_____
_____

Bolshevik Revolution:

_____
_____
_____
_____

Select one of the above events you believe to be a turning point in European history, then describe what it was like before and after that event.

Europe prior to the event:

_____
_____
_____
_____

Europe after the event:

_____
_____
_____
_____

Turning Point: Between the Wars

Give specific historical details about the three events listed below (e.g., who, what, when, where, why).

Hitler's Beer Hall Putsch:

_____

_____

_____

Stalin's Five-Year Plans:

_____

_____

_____

Great Terror in Soviet Union:

_____

_____

_____

Select one of the above events you believe to be a turning point in European history, then describe what it was like before and after that event.

Europe prior to the event:

_____

_____

_____

Europe after the event:

_____

_____

_____

Turning Point: WWII

Give specific historical details about the three events listed below (e.g., who, what, when, where, why).

Japanese Invasion of Manchuria:

_____

_____

_____

_____

German Invasion of Poland:

_____

_____

_____

_____

United States drops Atomic Bombs:

_____

_____

_____

_____

Select one of the above events you believe to be a turning point in European history, then describe what it was like before and after that event.

Europe prior to the event:

_____

_____

_____

_____

Europe after the event:

_____

_____

_____

_____

Turning Point: Cold War

Give specific historical details about the three events listed below (e.g., who, what, when, where, why).

Truman Doctrine:

_____
_____
_____
_____

Formation of NATO:

_____
_____
_____
_____

Building of Berlin Wall:

_____
_____
_____
_____

Select one of the above events you believe to be a turning point in European history, then describe what it was like before and after that event.

Europe prior to the event:

_____
_____
_____
_____

Europe after the event:

_____
_____
_____
_____

Turning Point: End of the Cold War

Give specific historical details about the three events listed below (e.g., who, what, when, where, why).

Vietnam War:

_____
_____
_____
_____

Détente:

_____
_____
_____
_____

Reunification of Germany:

_____
_____
_____
_____

Select one of the above events you believe to be a turning point in European history, then describe what it was like before and after that event.

Europe prior to the event:

_____
_____
_____
_____

Europe after the event:

_____
_____
_____
_____

Turning Point: Globalization and the West

Give specific historical details about the three events listed below (e.g., who, what, when, where, why).

Formation of OPEC:

_____

_____

_____

_____

Islamic Revolution in Iran:

_____

_____

_____

_____

9/11 Terrorist Attacks:

_____

_____

_____

_____

Select one of the above events you believe to be a turning point in European history, then describe what it was like before and after that event.

Europe prior to the event:

_____

_____

_____

_____

Europe after the event:

_____

_____

_____

_____

Student Instructions: Continuity and Change

When we are asked to identify continuity and change over time, we are asked to identify a series of events over a distinct time period in history. Normally these events are centered on a specific theme with defined start and end dates within that period.

The purpose of these Continuity and Change activities is to investigate a series of events, place them in chronological order, then determine whether there was either more continuity or change during that historical period. There is almost always a significant change within the period under investigation. As with all of the worksheets in this book, there are no right or wrong answers. The worksheets will hopefully provide you with opportunities to articulate arguments for class discussions.

The bottom part of the worksheet asks you to select the three events you feel are the most important, then narrow it down to one event, then articulate the reasons why you selected the event in question, and finally, to discuss what European history was like both before and after that event. Discussing what life was like both before and after the event is critical to finishing the task because it demonstrates a sophisticated understanding of the event under investigation.

Continuity and Change: Scientific Reason and Political Thought (1450–1750) (Example)

1450	1517	1450–1550	1532–33	1545–1563	17th Century	1642–51	1648	1750
High Renaissance Age of Humanism and changes to both art and literature Rise of new monarchs Rise of secular thought	Individualism brought about changes toward the Catholic Church, as Martin Luther posted his 95 theses.	New monarchs in Spain, England, and France	The Prince Act of Supremacy	Catholic Council of Trent	Scientific Revolution (Descartes and Bacon)	English Civil War (Hobbes's Leviathan)	Louis XIV	Enlightenment

- High Renaissance
- Age of Humanism and changes to both art and literature
- Rise of new monarchs
- Rise of secular thought

List three key dates/events from the timeline. Circle the most important one.

1450–Individualism   ⬭1543–Copernicus⬭   1750–Enlightenment

Characteristics of the history before: 1543

The status of European states was that of feudal order; it was a construct centralized by the Catholic Church. And though feudal monarchs aimed to take back power, it was a struggle that left new monarchs in a place of expansion but under the norm of the Church.

Characteristics of the history after: 1543

However, after the rise of the new sciences, which garnered new thought from the rise of the Protestant Reformation, European states grew to became more secular by 1750. It was the 1750 point that furthered the changes of the Renaissance, allowing for a later revolution in France.

Continuity and Change: Scientific Reason and Political Thought (1450–1750)

List three key dates/events from the timeline. Circle the most important one.

_____ _____ _____

Characteristics of the history before: _____

Characteristics of the history after: _____

Continuity and Change: European Atlantic Commerce and Expansion (1492–1763)

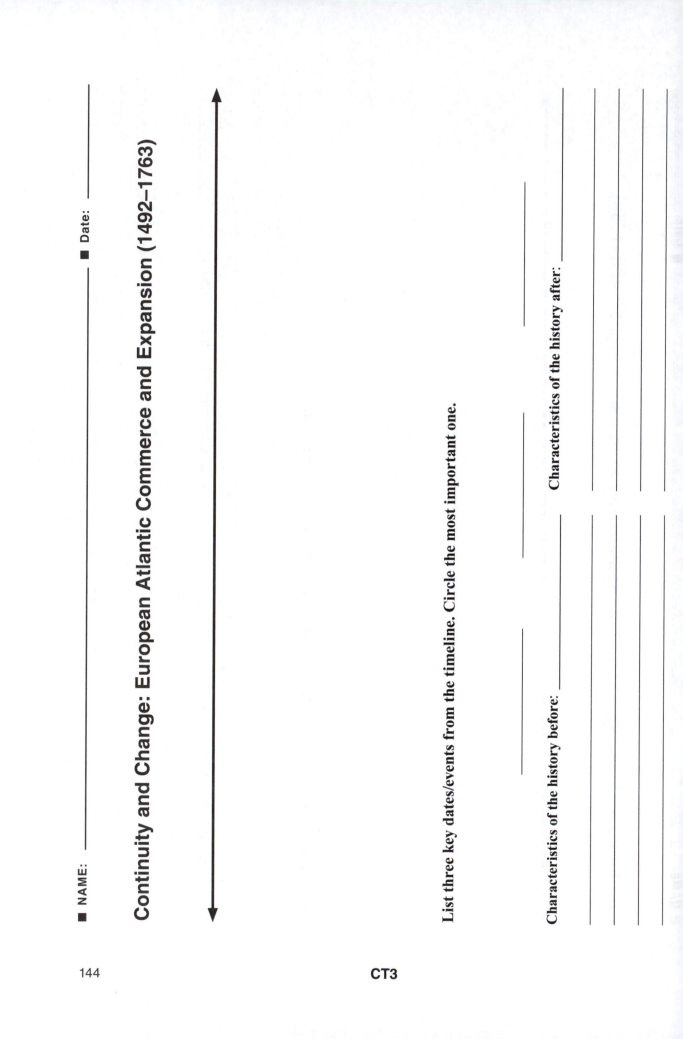

List three key dates/events from the timeline. Circle the most important one.

—————————— —————————— ——————————

Characteristics of the history before: ———

Characteristics of the history after: ———

——————————
——————————
——————————
——————————
——————————
——————————

CT3

Continuity and Change: Child-Rearing Beliefs and Practices (1525–1750)

List three key dates/events from the timeline. Circle the most important one.

_____   _____   _____

Characteristics of the history before:

_____

_____

_____

_____

_____

Characteristics of the history after:

_____

_____

_____

_____

_____

_____

CT4

145

Continuity and Change: European Attitudes toward Others (1500–1885)

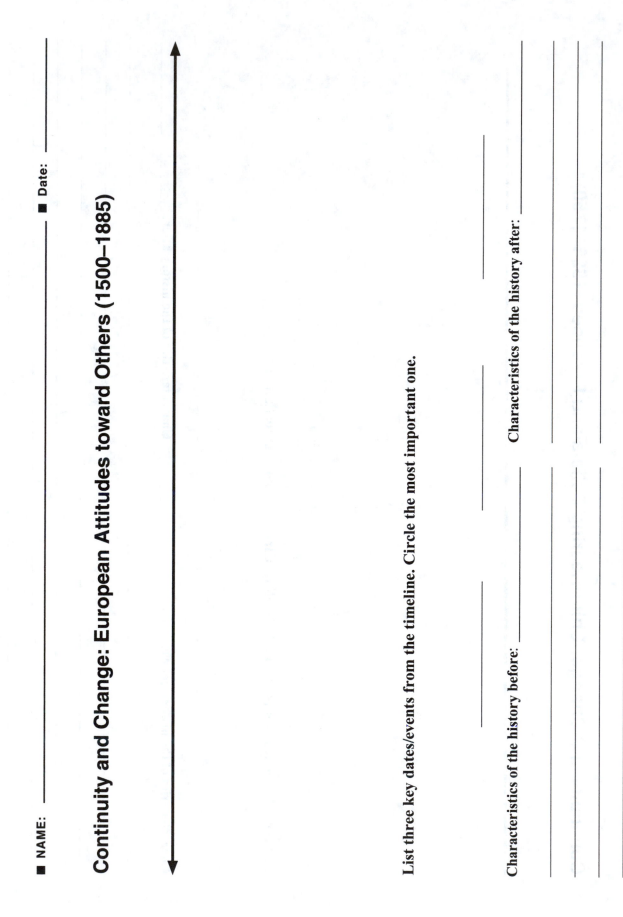

List three key dates/events from the timeline. Circle the most important one.

Characteristics of the history before: _____

Characteristics of the history after: _____

Continuity and Change: Religious Tolerance in Europe (1555–1715)

↕

List three key dates/events from the timeline. Circle the most important one.

_____   _____   _____

Characteristics of the history before: _____   **Characteristics of the history after:** _____

_____   _____

_____   _____

_____   _____

_____   _____

_____   _____

Continuity and Change: Urban Development during the 19th Century

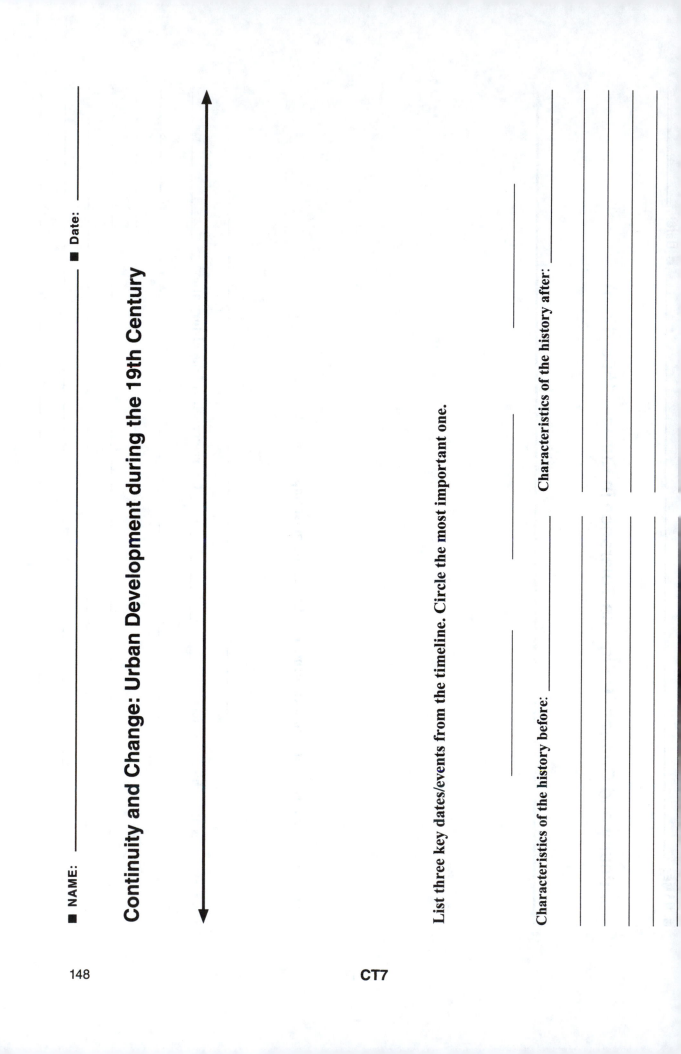

List three key dates/events from the timeline. Circle the **most important one.**

_____

_____

_____

Characteristics of the history before: _____

Characteristics of the history after: _____

Continuity and Change: Balance of Power (1701–1815)

List three key dates/events from the timeline. Circle the most important one.

Characteristics of the history before: _____

Characteristics of the history after: _____

Continuity and Change: Balance of Power (1815–1914)

List three key dates/events from the timeline. Circle the most important one.

_____   _____

Characteristics of the history before: _____

Characteristics of the history after: _____

_____

_____

_____

_____

_____

CT9

Continuity and Change: Art and Literature (1750–1900)

List three key dates/events from the timeline. Circle the most important one.

Characteristics of the history before: _____

Characteristics of the history after: _____

Continuity and Change: Women and Politics during the 20th Century

List three key dates/events from the timeline. Circle the most important one.

_____ _____ _____

Characteristics of the history before: _____

Characteristics of the history after: _____

CT11

Continuity and Change: Women and Politics (1750–1900)

List three key dates/events from the timeline. Circle the most important one.

_____

_____

_____

Characteristics of the history before: _____

Characteristics of the history after: _____

Continuity and Change: Organized Religion in Western Europe (1800–1920)

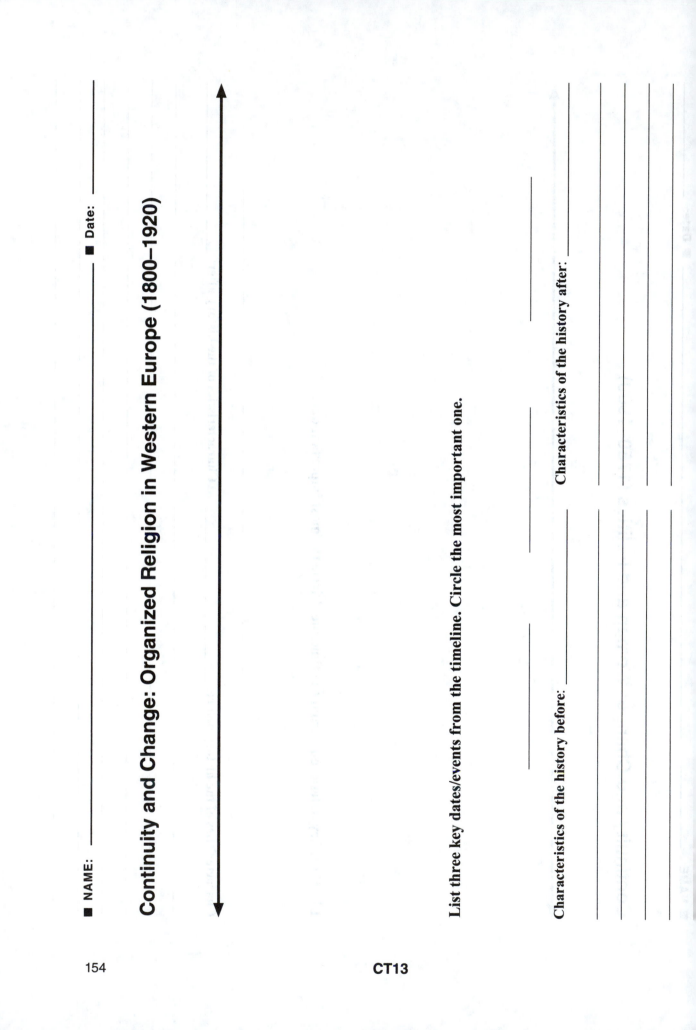

List three key dates/events from the timeline. Circle the most important one.

_____

_____

_____

Characteristics of the history before: _____

Characteristics of the history after: _____

154   **CT13**

Continuity and Change: European Balance of Power (1815–1871)

List three key dates/events from the timeline. Circle the most important one.

_____ _____ _____

Characteristics of the history before: _____

Characteristics of the history after: _____

Continuity and Change: Great Britain's Political Life (1830–1900)

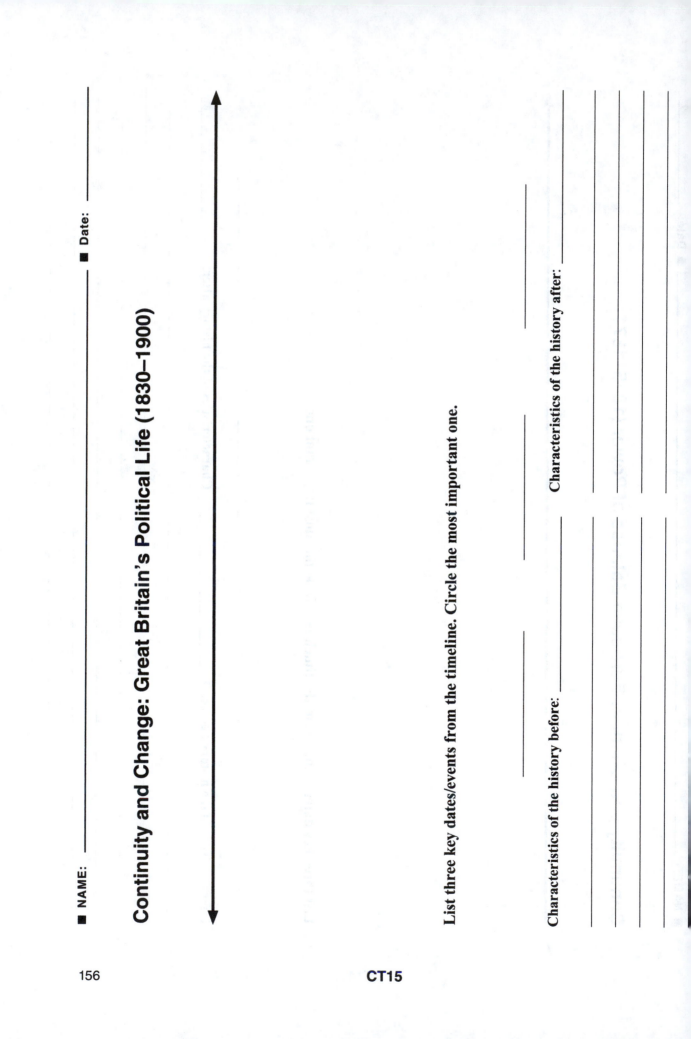

List three key dates/events from the timeline. Circle the most important one.

_____ _____ _____

Characteristics of the history before: _____

Characteristics of the history after: _____

CT15

Continuity and Change: European Life and Society (1850–1914)

List three key dates/events from the timeline. Circle the most important one.

Characteristics of the history before: _____

Characteristics of the history after: _____

Continuity and Change: Religion and Philosophy in France and Germany (1850–1950)

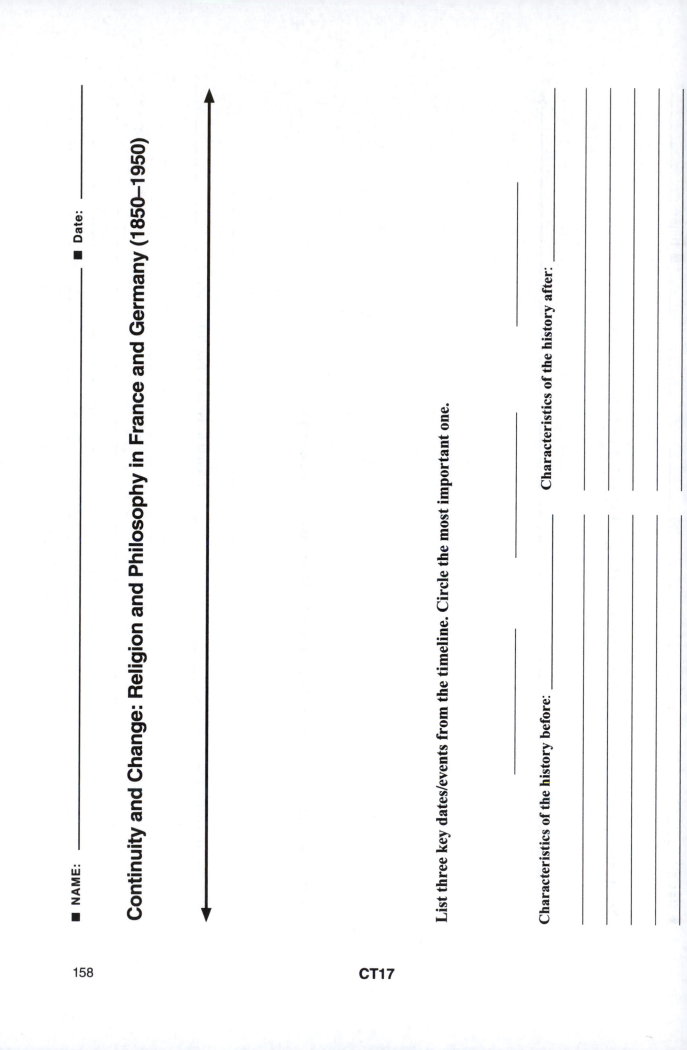

List three key dates/events from the timeline. Circle the most important one.

_____   _____   _____

Characteristics of the history before: _____

Characteristics of the history after: _____

_____
_____
_____
_____
_____
_____

CT17

Continuity and Change: Welfare State in Europe (1945–1991)

List three key dates/events from the timeline. Circle the most important one.

Characteristics of the history before: —————

Characteristics of the history after: —————

Continuity and Change: Mass Politics in Europe (1880–1939)

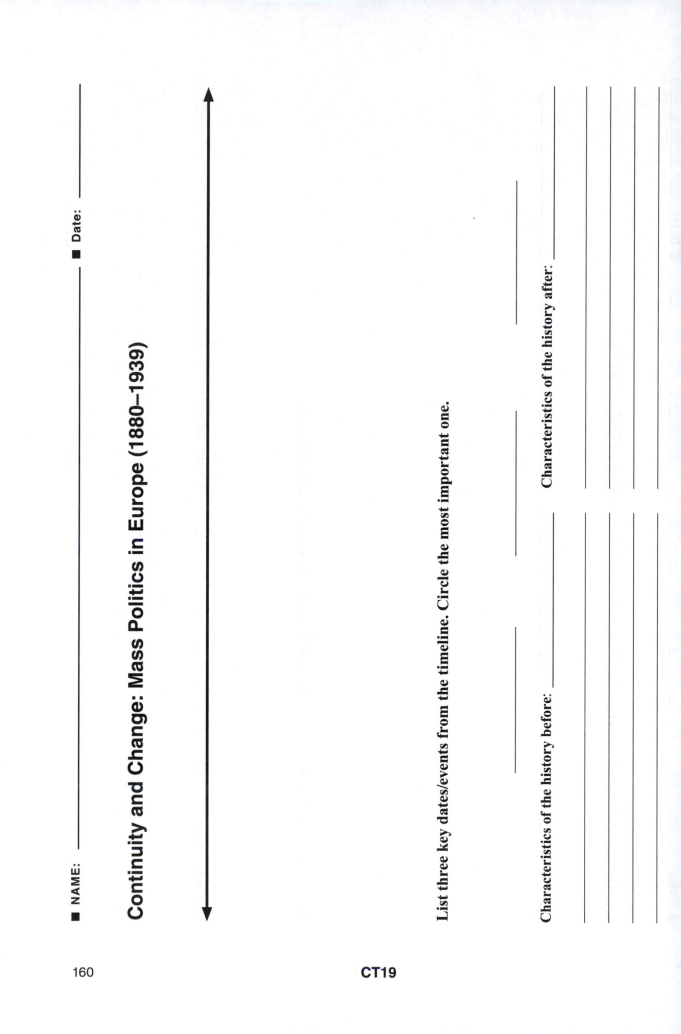

List three key dates/events from the timeline. Circle the most important one.

_____

_____

_____

Characteristics of the history before: _____

Characteristics of the history after: _____

CT19

Continuity and Change: European Attitudes toward the Poor (1750–1850)

↕

List three key dates/events from the timeline. Circle the most important one.

_____   _____   _____

Characteristics of the history before: _____

_____

_____

_____

_____

_____

Characteristics of the history after: _____

_____

_____

_____

_____

_____

Continuity and Change: European Family Life (1830–1900)

List three key dates/events from the timeline. Circle the most important one.

_____   _____   _____

Characteristics of the history before: _____

Characteristics of the history after: _____

CT21

Continuity and Change: Industrial Labor (1815–1900)

List three key dates/events from the timeline. Circle the most important one.

Characteristics of the history before: _____

Characteristics of the history after: _____

Continuity and Change: Soviet Union's Foreign and Domestic Policies (1945–1991)

List three key dates/events from the timeline. Circle the most important one.

Characteristics of the history before: _____

Characteristics of the history after: _____

Continuity and Change: Post-Contemporary Communist Europe (1991–2015)

List three key dates/events from the timeline. Circle the most important one.

_____   _____

Characteristics of the history before: Characteristics of the history after:

_____   _____

Student Instructions: Argumentation

When we are asked to construct a historical argument, we are asked to accumulate evidence and then to determine how it will be applied within the argument. The goal of historical argumentation is to convince an audience of the validity of our arguments.

The purpose of these Argumentation activities is to practice the necessary steps in constructing a valid argument. First, we must accumulate evidence that will support our arguments. Second, we must decide what evidence is compelling enough to side one way or the other on the topic at hand. Third, we must pick a side, and then begin the process of prewriting. If we do not want to pick a side, we have the option of modifying the prompt—that is, agreeing and disagreeing simultaneously. Fourth, we need to establish our thesis statement. The thesis statement is a critical part of the argument. It's a roadmap for our audience: Where are you going and what routes are you going to take to get there?

Argumentation: "The Renaissance was similar to the Middle Ages." (Example)

Support, modify, or refute this statement with specific historical evidence.

Middle Ages	Renaissance
• 2D art	• Women were more empowered
• Locked into a feudal class	• State usurped the Church
• Catholic Church at center	• 3D art
• Decentralized political systems	• Roman and Greek
• People faced disease and famine	• Vernacular
• Growth and expansion of towns	• Printing press
• Sovereign states	• Humanism
• Availability and growth of credit	• Rise of centralized states
• Growing population	• Increased skepticism
• Limited roles for women	• People still faced disease and famine
• Gothic	
• Latin	
• Scribes	

Thesis Statement:

Some scholars have long supported the notion that the period, known as the Renaissance, was a continuation of the Middle Ages; however, there is evidence that supports the claim that it was a different period. Looking at the works of historians, such as Jacob Burckhardt, one must refute the claim that the two periods were similar. Thus the change in state formation, the growth and change in emerging middle-class activities, and the new forms of art further illustrate this argument.

_____

_____

Argumentation: "The Renaissance was similar to the Middle Ages."

Support, modify, or refute this statement with specific historical evidence.

Thesis Statement:

_____

_____

_____

_____

_____

_____

_____

Argumentation: "Niccolo Machiavelli failed to develop new political theories."

Support, modify, or refute this statement with specific historical evidence.

Thesis Statement:

_____

_____

_____

_____

_____

_____

_____

Argumentation: "The visual arts of the 19th century were successful in challenging the institutional power of the Catholic Church."

Support, modify, or refute this statement with specific historical evidence.

Thesis Statement:

_____

_____

_____

_____

_____

_____

_____

Argumentation: "Alexander II's emancipation was a failed reform."

Support, modify, or refute this statement with specific historical evidence.

Thesis Statement:

_____

_____

_____

_____

_____

_____

_____

AR5

Argumentation: "Early 19th-century nationalists were at odds with Romanticism."

Support, modify, or refute this statement with specific historical evidence.

Thesis Statement:

_____ ___

_____

_____

_____

_____

_____

_____

_____

Argumentation: "Child-rearing practices and improved family views of the late 18th century have been exaggerated by historians."

Support, modify, or refute this statement with specific historical evidence.

Thesis Statement:

_____

_____

_____

_____

_____

_____

_____

Argumentation: "The burgeoning middle class sought transatlantic expansion and colonization more than European monarchs and the nobility."

Support, modify, or refute this statement with specific historical evidence.

Thesis Statement:

_____

_____

_____

_____

_____

_____

_____

Argumentation: "Martin Luther's *Against the Murdering, Thieving Hordes of Peasants* sought to advance his own movement."

Support, modify, or refute this statement with specific historical evidence.

Thesis Statement:

_____

_____

_____

_____

_____

_____

_____

Argumentation: "European monarchs impacted the spread of the Protestant Reformation."

Support, modify, or refute this statement with specific historical evidence.

Thesis Statement:

_____

_____

_____

_____

_____

_____

_____

Argumentation: "Eighteenth-century absolutists lacked absolute power over their subjects."

Support, modify, or refute this statement with specific historical evidence.

_____|_____

Thesis Statement:

_____

_____

_____

_____

_____

_____

_____

Argumentation: "Mikhail Gorbachev, not Ronald Reagan, brought an end to the Cold War."

Support, modify, or refute this statement with specific historical evidence.

Thesis Statement:

_____

_____

_____

_____

_____

_____

_____

Argumentation: "Economic pressures contributed to the advent of decolonization."

Support, modify, or refute this statement with specific historical evidence.

Thesis Statement:

_____

_____

_____

_____

_____

_____

_____

Argumentation: "Queen Elizabeth I of England empowered the middle class."

Support, modify, or refute this statement with specific historical evidence.

Thesis Statement:

_____

_____

_____

_____

_____

_____

_____

Argumentation: "Political, not religious, changes contributed to the witchcraft persecutions."

Support, modify, or refute this statement with specific historical evidence.

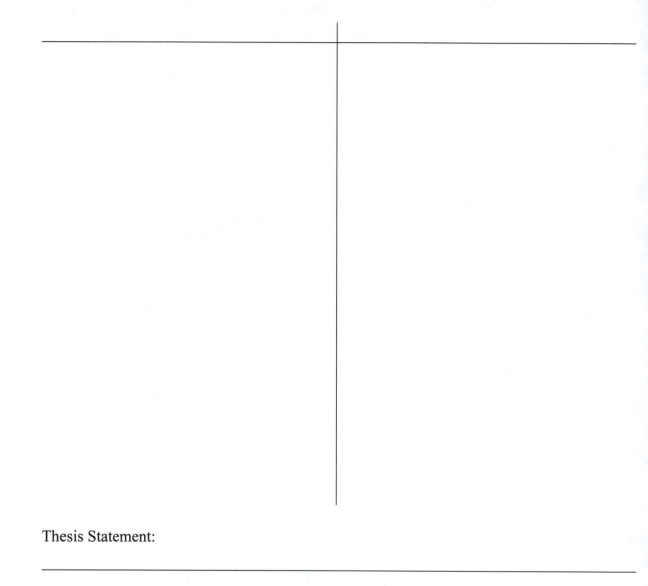

Thesis Statement:

_____

_____

_____

_____

_____

_____

_____

Argumentation: "The Thirty Years' War was a turning point in European history."

Support, modify, or refute this statement with specific historical evidence.

Thesis Statement:

_____

_____

_____

_____

_____

_____

_____

Argumentation: "The Enlightenment failed to improve the quality of life for the urban and rural poor."

Support, modify, or refute this statement with specific historical evidence.

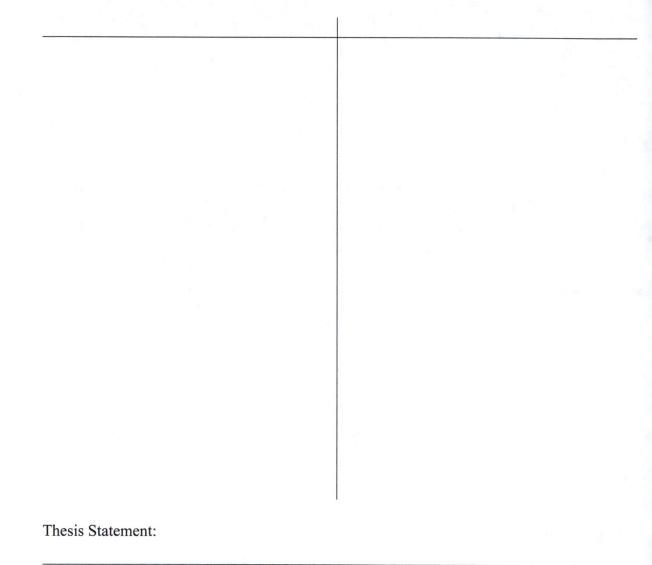

Thesis Statement:

_____
_____
_____
_____
_____
_____
_____

Argumentation: "Russia became a communist state under Joseph Stalin, not V.I. Lenin."

Support, modify, or refute this statement with specific historical evidence.

Thesis Statement:

_____

_____

_____

_____

_____

_____

_____

Argumentation: "Nationalism first emerged during the French Revolution."

Support, modify, or refute this statement with specific historical evidence.

Thesis Statement:

_____

_____

_____

_____

_____

_____

_____

Argumentation: "France during the Revolution of 1789 was the first atheist state in world history."

Support, modify, or refute this statement with specific historical evidence.

Thesis Statement:

_____

_____

_____

_____

_____

_____

_____

Argumentation: "Catherine the Great of Russia was the most enlightened despot."

Support, modify, or refute this statement with specific historical evidence.

Thesis Statement:

_____

_____

_____

_____

_____

_____

_____

Argumentation: "The Price Revolution was an inevitable consequence of a changing European economy."

Support, modify, or refute this statement with specific historical evidence.

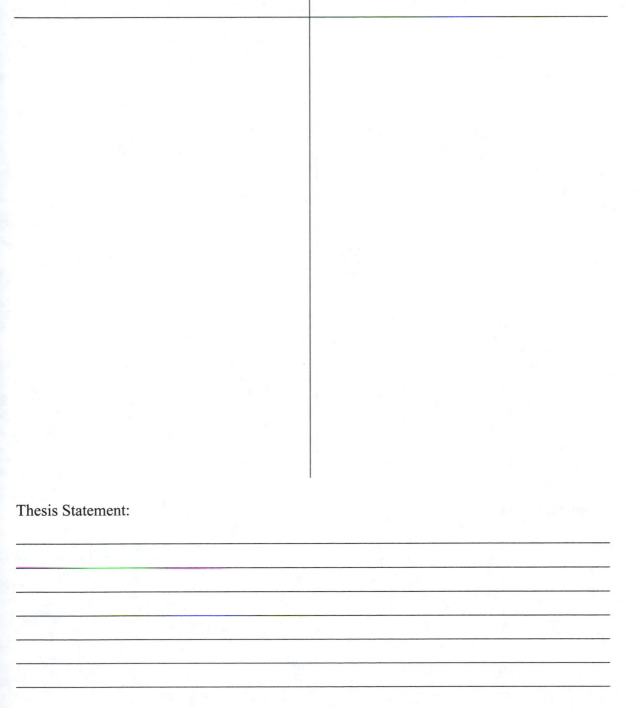

Thesis Statement:

_____

_____

_____

_____

_____

_____

Argumentation: "The European nobility exhibited absolute power from 1648 to 1815."

Support, modify, or refute this statement with specific historical evidence.

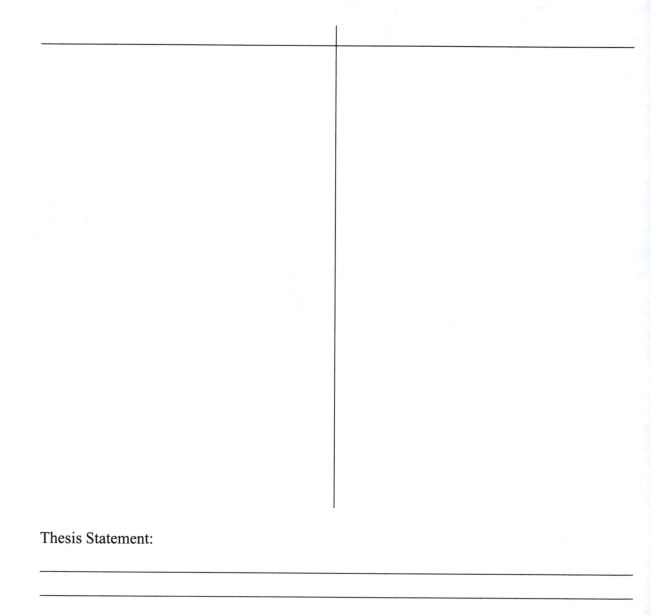

Thesis Statement:

_____

_____

_____

_____

_____

_____

_____

Argumentation: "The Congress of Vienna (1815) was a turning point in European history."

Support, modify, or refute this statement with specific historical evidence.

Thesis Statement:

_____

_____

_____

_____

_____

_____

_____

Argumentation: "The Cold War between the USSR and the United States was an inevitable conflict."

Support, modify, or refute this statement with specific historical evidence.

Thesis Statement:

_____

_____

_____

_____

_____

_____

_____

Argumentation: "Winston Churchill's response to the post–World War II economy contributed to his political demise."

Support, modify, or refute this statement with specific historical evidence.

Thesis Statement:

_____

_____

_____

_____

_____

_____

_____

Argumentation: "Margaret Thatcher's 'Iron Lady' title was misleading."

Support, modify, or refute this statement with specific historical evidence.

Thesis Statement:

_____

_____

_____

_____

_____

_____

_____

Argumentation: "The Cold War made the world safer."

Support, modify, or refute this statement with specific historical evidence.

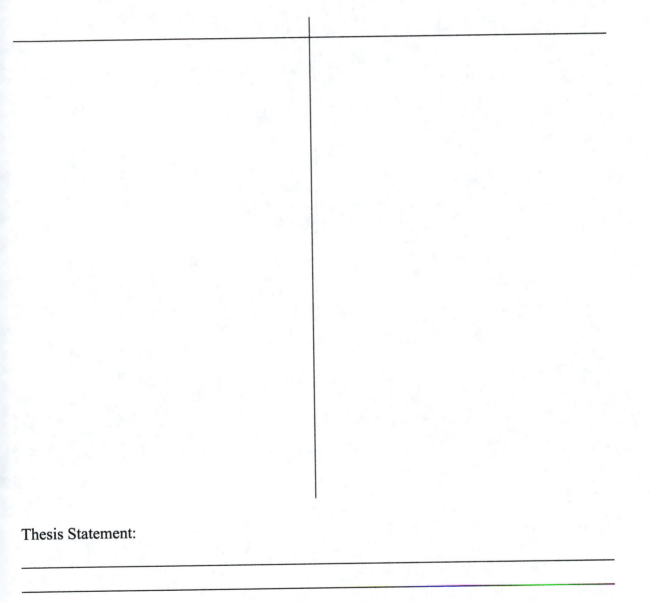

Thesis Statement:

_____

_____

_____

_____

_____

_____

_____

Argumentation: "Charles Darwin and Karl Marx symbolized a change in religious thought."

Support, modify, or refute this statement with specific historical evidence.

Thesis Statement:

_____

_____

_____

_____

_____

_____

_____

AR29

Argumentation: "The Balfour Declaration (1917) betrayed Palestinian sovereignty."

Support, modify, or refute this statement with specific historical evidence.

Thesis Statement:

_____

_____

_____

_____

_____

_____

_____

Argumentation: "Napoleon was a product of the Enlightenment."

Support, modify, or refute this statement with specific historical evidence.

Thesis Statement:

_____

_____

_____

_____

_____

_____

Student Instructions: Interpretation

When we are asked to make historical interpretations, we are asked to read and interpret excerpts from secondary sources. The difference between primary and secondary sources is the nature of when the excerpts were written. Primary sources are written by the historical figures under investigation. Secondary sources are written by historians about the historical figures under investigation. Sometimes secondary sources can become primary sources if the nature of the writing becomes so important that it lasts well into the future. Historical interpretation can involve either primary or secondary sources, but for the purposes of this workbook, we will strictly stick to secondary sources.

The purpose of these Interpretation activities is to practice reading a variety of small secondary excerpts from important historical scholarship, which is a challenging task. Historians are often products of their environment, thus the language can serve as a deterrent to the reader. If the language employs terms that are no longer part of the vernacular, then the meaning can be lost. Another reason this can be a challenging task is that historians often agree on something but disagree with regard to the importance of the event under investigation. For example, two historians may agree that the rise of the Nazi party in Germany was a bad thing, but they may disagree as to why it was bad. Since this is one of the primary purposes of historiography—that is, the interpretation and writing of historical events—it is important that we effectively engage secondary sources and interpret their different arguments.

Interpretation: The Crusades (Example)

'He who fights so the word of God may prevail is on the path of God.' The sentiments embodied in this saying attributed to Mohammad do much to explain the amazing success of Islam, which, through the zeal for jihad or holy war, extended from the borders of France to those of India by the early eighth century. Religious enthusiasm also lies behind the equally amazing accomplishments of the Christian warriors of the First Crusade. In both Moslem expansion and Christian conquest, however, luck was just as important as zeal. The Moslems were able to profit from the weaknesses of early seventh-century Christendom just as the crusaders, when they entered Jerusalem in bloody triumphs four and a half centuries later, were able to attribute their victory in part to dissension and weaknesses among the Moslems.—Ronald C. Finucane, *Soldiers of the Faith: Crusaders and Moslems at War*, 1983

Specific historical evidence to SUPPORT the interpretation above (not mentioned in passage):

By 1095, many Christians from various western kingdoms responded to Pope Urban II's call to recapture the holy land. This rush followed the Council of Clermont.

Specific historical evidence to SUPPORT the interpretation above (not mentioned in passage):

By 1099, Crusaders took the city of Jerusalem by exploiting the Muslims in population there.

Specific historical evidence to REFUTE the interpretation above (not mentioned in passage):

Both Muslims and Christians saw Jerusalem and its surrounding regions as holy to all groups. Many Muslims were open to Christians, often only using a jizya (tax) against them.

Interpretation: The Crusades

'He who fights so the word of God may prevail is on the path of God.' The sentiments embodied in this saying attributed to Mohammad do much to explain the amazing success of Islam, which, through the zeal for jihad or holy war, extended from the borders of France to those of India by the early eighth century. Religious enthusiasm also lies behind the equally amazing accomplishments of the Christian warriors of the First Crusade. In both Moslem expansion and Christian conquest, however, luck was just as important as zeal. The Moslems were able to profit from the weaknesses of early seventh-century Christendom just as the crusaders, when they entered Jerusalem in bloody triumphs four and a half centuries later, were able to attribute their victory in part to dissension and weaknesses among the Moslems.—Ronald C. Finucane, *Soldiers of the Faith: Crusaders and Moslems at War*, 1983

Specific historical evidence to SUPPORT the interpretation above (not mentioned in passage):

_____

_____

_____

_____

_____

Specific historical evidence to SUPPORT the interpretation above (not mentioned in passage):

_____

_____

_____

_____

_____

Specific historical evidence to REFUTE the interpretation above (not mentioned in passage):

_____

_____

_____

_____

_____

Interpretation: Columbus

Columbus was literally in the right place (Spain) at the right time to set his place in history. America was the right place at the right time to appropriate, simplify, and mould Columbus to reflect the image of an independent and growing America. Columbus is found throughout American popular culture, national commemorations and memory, and prominently in the Rotunda of the U.S. Capitol. Randolph Roger's massive bronze Columbus Doors express this vision of Columbus, the ultimate visual expression of America's self-identity as embodied in the explorer. He 'emerged from the shadows as a man and historical figure as he was a myth and symbol. He epitomized the explorer, the man of vision and audacity, the hero who overcame opposition and adversity to change history.'—Michael Kammen, "Mystic Chords of Memory," 1991

Columbus sent expedition after expedition into the interior. They found no gold fields, but had to fill up the ships returning to Spain with some kind of dividend. In the year 1495, they went on a great slave raid, rounded up fifteen hundred Arawak men, women, and children, put them in pens guarded by Spaniards and dogs, then picked the five hundred best specimens to load onto ships. Of those five hundred, two hundred died en route. The rest arrived alive in Spain and were put up for sale by the archdeacon of the town, who reported that, although the slaves were "naked as the day they were born," they showed "no more embarrassment than animals."—Howard Zinn, *A People's History of the United States*, 2005

Specific historical evidence to SUPPORT the interpretation above (not mentioned in passage):

_____

_____

_____

_____

_____

Specific historical evidence to SUPPORT the interpretation above (not mentioned in passage):

_____

_____

_____

_____

_____

Specific historical evidence to REFUTE the interpretation above (not mentioned in passage):

_____

_____

_____

_____

_____

IN3

Interpretation: Men and Women in the Renaissance

Many things conspired to give leadership and acclaim in education and letters to the women of Italy, earlier than to women of other countries. Italy was the original home of the revival of the Latin classics and it was to Italy that the choicest of Greek classics were brought from Byzantium, before and after the fall of Constantinople to the Turks . . . With the revival of classical learning came the humanizing of intellectual interest, knowledge, and public measures; that is, thought and action were directed by this learning to human concerns . . . Now Italian men and women were in possession of literary and philosophic works dealing entirely with the great human and nature subjects . . . Italian men and women now had models of writing by Greek and Roman thinkers and stylists, inviting them to lofty aspirations and lucid expressions whether in poetry, letters, the arts, history, philosophy, or politics. . . . The number of women who devoted themselves to scholarship was by no means as large as the number of men, for reasons other than the lack of talents; but in the fifteenth century and early sixteenth century many Italian women displayed the highest technical competence in the study, interpretation, and exposition of the revived humanist learning.—Mary R. Beard, *Women as Force in History: A Study in Traditions and Realities*, 1946

Italy was well in advance of the rest of Europe from roughly 1350 to 1530 because of its early consolidation of genuine states, the mercantile and manufacturing economy that supported them, and its working out of postfeudal and even postguild social relations. These developments reorganized Italian society along modern lines and opened the possibilities for the social and cultural expression for which the age is known. Yet precisely these developments affected women adversely, so much so that there was no Renaissance for women . . . The state, early capitalism, and the social relations formed by them impinged on the lives of Renaissance women in different ways according to their different positions in society. But the startling fact is that women as a group, especially among the classes that dominated Italian urban life, experienced a contradiction of social and personal options that men of their classes either did not, as was the case with the bourgeoisie, or did not experience as markedly, as was the case with the nobility.—Joan Kelly-Gadol, "Did Women Have a Renaissance?," 1987

Specific historical evidence to SUPPORT the interpretation above (not mentioned in passage):

_____

_____

_____

_____

_____

Specific historical evidence to SUPPORT the interpretation above (not mentioned in passage):

_____

_____

_____

_____

_____

Specific historical evidence to REFUTE the interpretation above (not mentioned in passage):

_____

_____

_____

_____

_____

Interpretation: Renaissance

The soul of Western Christendom itself was outgrowing medieval forms and modes of thought that had become shackles. The Middle Ages had always lived in the shadow of Antiquity, always handled its treasures, or what they had of them, interpreting it according to truly medieval principles: scholastic theology and chivalry, asceticism and courtesy. Now, by an inward ripening, the mind, after having been so long conversant with the forms of Antiquity, began to grasp its spirit. The incomparable simpleness and purity of the ancient culture, its exactitude of conception and of expression, its easy and natural thought and strong interest in men and in life, all this began to dawn upon men's minds. Europe, after having lived in the shadow of Antiquity, lived in its sunshine once more.—Johan Huizinga, *The Waning of the Middle Ages*, 1948

Specific historical evidence to SUPPORT the interpretation above (not mentioned in passage):

_____

_____

_____

_____

_____

Specific historical evidence to SUPPORT the interpretation above (not mentioned in passage):

_____

_____

_____

_____

_____

Specific historical evidence to REFUTE the interpretation above (not mentioned in passage):

_____

_____

_____

_____

_____

Interpretation: Reformation

The Reformation grew out of the depths of a church that sacramentally and legally embraced all of society. If the progress of this movement was shaped by the social–political currents of the age, its points of origin is to be found in a question of authority raised by a troubled conscience and not in particular abuses. The late medieval church, through a process of excessive institutionalization, had sacrificed spirit to structure and had come to confuse authority with its own practiced and judgments. Confusions over the actual tradition of the church was aggravated in the schools by the rending of scripture into a collection of arguments and propositions for philosophical inquiry. In each process scripture, the ultimate source of knowledge of the faith, had lost its unity and integrity.—John M. Headley, "The Continental Reformation: A Religious Interpretation," 1971

The Reformation was successful beyond the dreams of earlier potentially similar, movements not so much because the time was ripe for it, but rather because it found favor with the secular arm. Desire for Church lands, resistance to Imperial and papal claims, the ambition to create self-contained and independent states, all played their part in this, but so quite often did a genuine attachment to the teaching of the reformers. [. . .] The tenet rested on simple fact: as long as membership of a secular polity involved membership of an ecclesiastical organization, religious dissent stood equal to political disaffection and even treason. Hence governments enforced uniformity, and hence the religion of the ruler was that of its country.—G. R. Elton, "A Political Interpretation of the Reformation," 1958

Specific historical evidence to SUPPORT the interpretation above (not mentioned in passage):

_____

_____

_____

_____

_____

Specific historical evidence to SUPPORT the interpretation above (not mentioned in passage):

_____

_____

_____

_____

_____

Specific historical evidence to REFUTE the interpretation above (not mentioned in passage):

_____

_____

_____

_____

_____

IN6

Interpretation: Martin Luther's Reforms

It has been said that 'they who do not rightly estimate the Reformation cannot rightly understand Luther, since Luther apart from the Reformation would cease to be Luther.' This certainly is true, but no less true is it that apart from Luther the Reformation itself cannot be understood. He is its key figure, protagonist and spokesman alike, upon all others zealous for change were more or less dependent. Indeed, whether but for Luther the Reform movement of the sixteenth century would have swept over Europe in the way it did is highly questionable. What he achieved was rendered possible because the time and the milieu were matched in him by the man also, so that all the necessary elements were present to issue in events such as, in the most authentic sense, were epoch-making. That achievement was not therefore something external to him, but the utterance of the man himself and of his profound personal experience. Over the preceding century voices had repeatedly called for the reform of abuses and corruptions, but there had emerged no guiding principle on which Reformation could successfully be carried through, nor a dominant personality to give it impetus.—Bernard M. G. Reardon, *Religious Thought in the Reformation*, 1995

I believe that Luther represents a catastrophe in the history of Western civilization. This is not to say that the catastrophe was all his fault. All sides have a share of blame in the boiling hatreds and carnage that consumed Europe for well over a century after Luther died. But in my view, whatever good Luther did is not matched by the calamities that came because of him. . . . We know now that things can go terribly and catastrophically wrong and that all the good that comes from great events does not necessarily or even usually overbalance the evil. Some good came from the Reformation as Luther shaped it, but I remain convinced that our world would have been far better off had events taken a different course.—Richard Marius, *Martin Luther: The Christian Between God and Death*, 1999

Specific historical evidence to SUPPORT the interpretation above (not mentioned in passage):

_____

_____

_____

_____

_____

Specific historical evidence to SUPPORT the interpretation above (not mentioned in passage):

_____

_____

_____

_____

_____

Specific historical evidence to REFUTE the interpretation above (not mentioned in passage):

_____

_____

_____

_____

Interpretation: Reformation and Authority

Up to the Peasants' Revolt the Reformation in Germany was a spontaneous folk movement. Like freshet winds of springtime the Reformation streamed over Germany. With its own young strength, the new evangelism conquered wide parts of the land. Preachers suddenly appearing in German cities brought the Word of God in Luther's understanding down to the common man. . . . In the beginning there was something elemental about the Reformation. It had nothing to do with those who ruled. The Word of God spread and grew whether or not the authorities gave it room or hindered its course. Nevertheless this springtime of reformation . . . came to an end with the Peasants' Revolt. Henceforth the Reformation was not of the people. Now suddenly reformation came to be relished by the authorities.—Franz Lau, "Did Popular Reformation Really Stop with the Peasants' Defeat?," 1968

Specific historical evidence to SUPPORT the interpretation above (not mentioned in passage):

_____
_____
_____
_____
_____

Specific historical evidence to SUPPORT the interpretation above (not mentioned in passage):

_____
_____
_____
_____
_____

Specific historical evidence to REFUTE the interpretation above (not mentioned in passage):

_____
_____
_____
_____
_____

Interpretation: Calvin and Calvinism

But if the sovereign is not a monarch, what must he be? A magistrate elected by the people. Calvin was as much in favor of the democratic form as he was opposed to the monarchical one. . . . Is it necessary to recall the constant and pointed lessons in real democracy that Calvin's discipline gave every day? These were lessons not in egalitarianism but in the principle of equality before the law.—Emile Doumergue, *Jean Calvin*, 1917

It is not difficult to notice that Calvinist religious society . . . far from being, as some imagine, the 'cradle of modern ideas,' represented rather a retrogression in respect to the political society that had seen its birth. Calvin did not wish to give his Church even the slightly democratic institutions of sixteenth-century Geneva.—Georges de Lagarde, *Research on the Political Spirit of the Reformation*, 1926

Specific historical evidence to SUPPORT the interpretation above (not mentioned in passage):

_____

_____

_____

_____

_____

Specific historical evidence to SUPPORT the interpretation above (not mentioned in passage):

_____

_____

_____

_____

_____

Specific historical evidence to REFUTE the interpretation above (not mentioned in passage):

_____

_____

_____

_____

_____

Interpretation: John Wyclif and the Reformation

John Wyclif has sometimes been viewed as a forerunner of the Reformation of the sixteenth century because his arguments attacked the foundations of the medieval Catholic Church's organization and practices. His attacks on church property were especially popular, and he attracted a number of followers who came to be known as Lollards. Persecution by royal and church authorities who feared the socioeconomic consequences of Wyclif's ideas forced the Lollards to go underground after 1400. —Jackson Spielvogel, *Western Civilization*, 2006

John Wyclif, a theologian of Oxford University, first became prominent around 1375 for attacking the wealth and luxury of the church and for maintaining that all church property was held only at the discretion of the secular authorities. At this time, a group of English nobles headed by John of Ghent, duke of Lancaster, were looking with greedy eyes on the possessions of the church and were delighted to find an ecclesiastical supporter. Wyclif was lucky in having the protection of the powerful duke of Lancaster for the rest of his life.—Brian Tierney, *Western Europe in the Middle Ages: 300 to 1475*, 1970

Specific historical evidence to SUPPORT the interpretation above (not mentioned in passage):

_____

_____

_____

_____

_____

Specific historical evidence to SUPPORT the interpretation above (not mentioned in passage):

_____

_____

_____

_____

_____

Specific historical evidence to REFUTE the interpretation above (not mentioned in passage):

_____

_____

_____

_____

_____

Interpretation: Religion and Capitalism

Striving for wealth is objectionable only when it has the aim of a carefree and merry existence. But as exercise of duty in a calling it is not only morally permitted but actually commanded . . . Worldly Protestant asceticism acted effectively against the spontaneous enjoyment of wealth; it limited consumption, especially that of luxuries. On the other hand, it eliminated traditional inhibitions against the acquisition of property; it burst the bonds of the profit motive by not only legalizing it, but even viewing it as directly willed by God . . . He desired rational and utilitarian use of wealth for the purposes of the individual and the community.—Max Weber, *The Protestant Ethic and the Spirit of Capitalism*, 1905

A reasonable estimate of economic organization must allow for the fact that, unless industry is to be paralyzed by recurrent revolts on the part of outraged human nature, it must satisfy criteria which are not purely economic... natural appetites may be purified or restrained, as, in fact, in some considerable measure they already have been, by being submitted to the control of some larger body of interest.—R.H. Tawney, *Religion and the Rise of Capitalism*, 1926

Specific historical evidence to SUPPORT the interpretation above (not mentioned in passage):

_____

_____

_____

_____

_____

Specific historical evidence to SUPPORT the interpretation above (not mentioned in passage):

_____

_____

_____

_____

_____

Specific historical evidence to REFUTE the interpretation above (not mentioned in passage):

_____

_____

_____

_____

_____

Interpretation: West Africa Slave Trade and British Capitalism

[F]or historians of the industrial revolution, British involvement in the Atlantic slave trade brings forth, at most, a proper and perfunctory moral abhorrence. It plays no part in the stories they weave about the origins of the industrial revolution. What accounts for the muteness of the economic historians of the industrial revolution on the slave trade and slavery in their analyses of British industrialization? Has there been a conspiracy of silence . . . [or] has it simply been a more innocent oversight among a group of scholars so passionately engaged in supporting or debunking one another's pet explanations for the rise of British industry that they have failed to consider explanations put forward by other outside their loop? The polite explanation is, of course, that the historians of the industrial revolution have a valid reason for not mentioning arguments that assign a leading role in British industrial expansion to the foreign sector and, more specifically, to the slave trade and plantation slavery . . . For them, commerce with the colonial plantations and with the African coastal regions was no more than a handmaiden to the British process of industrialization, and a minor handmaiden at that—so minor that it can be ignored.—William Darity, Jr., "British Industry and the West Indies Plantations," 1990

Specific historical evidence to SUPPORT the interpretation above (not mentioned in passage):

_____

_____

_____

_____

_____

Specific historical evidence to SUPPORT the interpretation above (not mentioned in passage):

_____

_____

_____

_____

_____

Specific historical evidence to REFUTE the interpretation above (not mentioned in passage):

_____

_____

_____

_____

_____

Interpretation: Abolition and Slavery

The philosophy of benevolence was a product of the seventeenth century, when certain British Protestants, shaken by theological controversy and the implications of modern science, looked increasingly to human nature and conduct as a basis of faith. In their impatience with theological dogma, their distaste for the doctrine of original sin, their appreciation for human feeling and sentiment, and their confidence in man's capacity for moral improvement, these Latitudinarians, as they were called, anticipated the main concerns of the Enlightenment, and laid an indispensable foundation for social reform.—David Brion Davis, *The Problems of Slavery in the Age of Revolution, 1770–1823*, 1975

Specific historical evidence to SUPPORT the interpretation above (not mentioned in passage):

_____

_____

_____

_____

_____

Specific historical evidence to SUPPORT the interpretation above (not mentioned in passage):

_____

_____

_____

_____

_____

Specific historical evidence to REFUTE the interpretation above (not mentioned in passage):

_____

_____

_____

_____

_____

Interpretation: Scientific Revolution

Before the seventeenth century had opened, the general state of knowledge in regard to the physical universe had been conducive to the production of a number of speculative systems—these not founded upon scientific enquiry as a rule, but generally compounded out of ingredients taken from classical antiquity. Already in the sixteenth century, also, attention had been directed to the question of a general scientific method, and in the seventeenth century this problem of method came to be one of the grand preoccupations, not merely of the practicing scientist, but, at a higher level, amongst the general thinkers and philosophers.—Herbert Butterfield, *The Origins of Modern Science, 1300–1800*, 1957

As our understanding of science in the seventeenth century has changed in recent years, so historians have become increasingly uneasy with the very idea of "the Scientific Revolution." Even the legitimacy of each word making up that phrase has been individually contested. Many historians are now no longer satisfied that there was a singular and discrete event, localized in time and space, that can be pointed to as "the" Scientific Revolution. Such historians now reject even the notion that there was any single coherent cultural entity called "science" in the seventeenth century to undergo revolutionary change. There was, rather, a diverse array of cultural practices aimed at understanding, explaining, and controlling the natural world, each with different characteristics and each experiencing different modes of change. . . . And many historians do not now accept that the changes wrought on scientific beliefs and practices during the seventeenth century were as "revolutionary" as has been widely portrayed. The continuity of seventeenth-century natural philosophy with its medieval past is now routinely asserted.—Steven Shapin, *The Scientific Revolution*, 1996

Specific historical evidence to SUPPORT the interpretation above (not mentioned in passage):

_____

_____

_____

_____

_____

Specific historical evidence to SUPPORT the interpretation above (not mentioned in passage):

_____

_____

_____

_____

_____

Specific historical evidence to REFUTE the interpretation above (not mentioned in passage):

_____

_____

_____

_____

Interpretation: Scientific Revolution II

The Middle Ages were the age of faith, and to that extent they were unfavorable to scientific speculation. It is not that scientists as such were proscribed. For on the whole the persecution of men for their scientific ideas was very rare: rare because men with dangerous ideas, or indeed with any scientific ideas at all, were themselves very rare; and it is indeed surprising that there were any at all. This does not mean that there were no intellectual giants. All it means is that in an age which was one of faith, men of intellectual and spirit found the calls of faith itself—its elucidation, its controversies, and its conquests—a task sufficient to absorb them. To put it simply, they had no time for occupation like science.—Michael Postan, "Why Was Science Backward in the Middle Ages?," 1973

There were an infinite number of motives which led men to engage in scientific work and to clear the scientific point of view from encumbrances; but we may group together some of the most important under general headings, always remembering in actual life each of them was compounded with others. There were economic motives. . . . Not far removed from the economic motives were those of the physicians and surgeons, who revolutionized anatomy and physiology. . . . It was a pope who presided over the astronomical researchers by which the calendar was reformed in the sixteenth century. Deeper and stronger was the desire to study the wonders of science, and the order which it unraveled in the universe, as manifestations of the Creator's will.—Sir George Clark, "Early Modern Europe: Motives for the Scientific Revolution," 1957

Specific historical evidence to SUPPORT the interpretation above (not mentioned in passage):

_____

_____

_____

_____

Specific historical evidence to SUPPORT the interpretation above (not mentioned in passage):

_____

_____

_____

_____

_____

Specific historical evidence to REFUTE the interpretation above (not mentioned in passage):

_____

_____

_____

_____

_____

Interpretation: Early Modern Child Rearing

Between the end of the Middle Ages and the seventeenth century, the child had won a place beside his parents to which he could not lay claim at a time when it was customary to entrust him to strangers. This return of the children to the home was a great event: it gave the seventeenth-century family its principal characteristic, which distinguished it from the medieval family. The child became an indispensable element of everyday life, and his parents worried about his education, his career, his future. He was not yet the pivot of the whole system, but he had become a much more important character.
—Philippe Ariès, *Centuries of Childhood*, 1962

Specific historical evidence to SUPPORT the interpretation above (not mentioned in passage):

_____

_____

_____

_____

_____

Specific historical evidence to SUPPORT the interpretation above (not mentioned in passage):

_____

_____

_____

_____

_____

Specific historical evidence to REFUTE the interpretation above (not mentioned in passage):

_____

_____

_____

_____

_____

Interpretation: Enlightenment and Its Influences

But here is the wonder; here and only here we are deceived. This powerful apparatus of defense defending nothing, nothing but emptiness and negation. There was nothing behind it to love, nothing to hold and cling to. This dogmatic reason was the repudiation of all faith, this tyrannical liberty the denial of all law. I shall not stress the criticism so often leveled at the philosophes; they themselves admitted and glorified the nihilism of their ideals. . . . What did they do in this republic? Nothing, after all, but what occurred in [the] salon; they talked. They were there to talk, not to act. All this intellectual agitation, this immense exchange of speeches, writings and correspondence was not directed toward the slightest product or practical effort. It was merely a question of "concurrence of ideas," of "union for truth."—Augustin Cochin, "The Subversive Influence of the Philosophes and the Sociétés de Pensée," 1921

This vast, vigorous and spirited awakening of intellectual interests was not limited to Paris or a few great cities. It belonged to all France, that is, the French middle classes since we have no means of penetrating the minds of the workers and peasants for whom the struggle to live was too great to permit them to speculate or even to read. . . . Everywhere on the eve of the Revolution there were thinking minds or at least those that sought to think. . . . One gains the same impression when one considers the role of the great writers. Certainly it was considerable. . . . Even in the mere posters in the provinces, it was these writers who were appealed to and cited.—Daniel Mornet, *French Thought in the Eighteenth Century*, 1929

Specific historical evidence to SUPPORT the interpretation above (not mentioned in passage):

_____

_____

_____

_____

_____

Specific historical evidence to SUPPORT the interpretation above (not mentioned in passage):

_____

_____

_____

_____

_____

Specific historical evidence to REFUTE the interpretation above (not mentioned in passage):

_____

_____

_____

_____

Interpretation: Rise of Great Powers

As Europe came to be ruled by great military states, those states had to act increasingly in terms of state interest. The great political problems that grew out of the decay of the Holy Roman and Spanish empires seemed to reflect dynastic politics, but in the actual course of events, political realities based upon military, commercial, and financial considerations, became the predominant counters. The rise of great standing armies and their maintenance in the field made strenuous demands upon the treasury and the credit of the kings. In order to assure a continuous flow of revenue from taxation, required to meet the mounting costs, governments had to formulate and implement policies that would increase the riches of their potential taxpayers, and officials primarily interested in maintaining the power of their state inevitably urged policies that coincided with state interest. European governments were assuming a characteristically modern shape and thereby rendering dynastic politics altogether anachronistic.—John B. Wolf, *The Emergence of the Great Powers, 1685–1715*, 1951

To justify policies on the basis of a state's national honor, reputation and prestige is still very much the norm. . . . In an age when rulers looked on their states as their personal family property, it was inevitable that they should stress their personal honor, reputation and prestige. This also explains why most international disputes tended to be over dynastic claims. Dynasticism was a dominant theme in international relations throughout the seventeenth and eighteenth centuries.—Derek McKay and H.M. Scott, *The Rise of the Great Powers 1648–1815*, 1983

Specific historical evidence to SUPPORT the interpretation above (not mentioned in passage):

_____

_____

_____

_____

_____

Specific historical evidence to SUPPORT the interpretation above (not mentioned in passage):

_____

_____

_____

_____

_____

Specific historical evidence to REFUTE the interpretation above (not mentioned in passage):

_____

_____

_____

_____

_____

Interpretation: Aristocracy and Peasants

By 1700 grammar schools and universities were no longer crowded with gentlemen's sons; indeed they were emptying fast (Christ's College, Cambridge, had only three freshmen in 1733, and many of its rooms were deserted). Shopkeepers preferred the new education provided by private enterprise, the schools and academies which taught bookkeeping, languages, geography, navigation—the arts necessary for commercial life; gentlemen sent their sons abroad on a Grand Tour. By 1720, no Englishman or German pretending to a place in society could expect to be regarded as anything but country bumpkin unless he spent two or three years in France or Italy.—J.H. Plumb, "The Cosmopolitan Aristocracy," 1963

Schooling for most peasants was, at best, pitifully inadequate and usually entirely absent, even where laws declared elementary education compulsory . . . [B]y far the greatest part of Europe's peasantry lived out their lives in darkest ignorance. The peasants themselves, oppressed, contemned, and kept in ignorance by their social betters, accepted the stamp of inferiority pressed upon them. "I am only a serf" the peasant would reply when asked to identify himself. They seemed without pride or self-respect, dirty, lazy, crafty, and always suspicious of their masters and of the world they that lay outside their village.—Jerome Blum, "Lords and Peasants," 1978

Specific historical evidence to SUPPORT the interpretation above (not mentioned in passage):

_____

_____

_____

_____

_____

Specific historical evidence to SUPPORT the interpretation above (not mentioned in passage):

_____

_____

_____

_____

_____

Specific historical evidence to REFUTE the interpretation above (not mentioned in passage):

_____

_____

_____

_____

IN19

Interpretation: Cause of the French Revolution

Some historians have noted that differences between aristocrats and bourgeoisie, and within both social groups, had become considerably blurred during the eighteenth century; that most of the bourgeois members of the Estate-General were not drawn from commerce and manufacturing but rather from law, and that, in any case, the upper middle class and nobles by the time of the Revolution shared a common obsession with money, not privilege. Thus one cannot accurately depict the Revolution as having been simply a victory for the bourgeois. Moreover, revisionists have argued that the Revolution did not expedite capitalism but even retarded it, by launching France and Europe into a long series of costly wars.—John Merriman, *A History of Modern Europe: From the Renaissance to the Present*, 1996

The ultimate cause of the French Revolution of 1789 goes deep into the history of France. At the end of the eighteenth century the social structure of France was aristocratic. It showed the traces of having originated at a time when land was almost the only form of wealth, and when the possessors of land were masters of those who needed it to work and to live. It is true that in the course of age-old struggles the king had been able gradually to deprive the lords of their political power and subject nobles and clergy to his authority. But he had left the first place in the second hierarchy. Still restless at being merely his "subjects," they remained privileged persons.—Georges Lefebvre, *The Coming of the French Revolution*, 1947

Specific historical evidence to SUPPORT the interpretation above (not mentioned in passage):

_____

_____

_____

_____

_____

Specific historical evidence to SUPPORT the interpretation above (not mentioned in passage):

_____

_____

_____

_____

_____

Specific historical evidence to REFUTE the interpretation above (not mentioned in passage):

_____

_____

_____

_____

_____

Interpretation: French Revolution

A new France was born during those four years of revolution. For the first time in centuries the peasant ate his fill, straightened his back and dared to speak out. . . . It was owing to this new birth that France was able to maintain her wars under the Republic of Napoleon, and to carry the principles of the Great Revolution into [other countries]. . . . The self-contained energy was such in villages regenerated by the Revolution, that in a few years France became a country of well-to-do peasants, and her enemies soon discovered in spite of all the blood she had shed and the losses she had sustained, France, in respect of her productivity, was the richest country in Europe. . . . Such was the effect of the Revolution.—Peter Kropotkin, *The Great French Revolution, 1789–1793*, 1971

Specific historical evidence to SUPPORT the interpretation above (not mentioned in passage):

_____

_____

_____

_____

_____

Specific historical evidence to SUPPORT the interpretation above (not mentioned in passage):

_____

_____

_____

_____

_____

Specific historical evidence to REFUTE the interpretation above (not mentioned in passage):

_____

_____

_____

_____

_____

Interpretation: French Revolution II

The principle of liberty and the proposition that all men are created equal were inherited by the people of the United States from a long tradition. That tradition had Biblical origins; its genealogy can easily be traced by the brilliant pattern it weaves through the history of British and European political philosophy and constitutional practice. Its collateral American lines reached maturity in the constitutions of the separate states, . . . the Declaration of Independence itself, and in the first ten amendments of the federal constitution. . . . It is sometimes believed that it was because of the principles for which the Americans fought and which they had incorporated in their widely admired Declaration of Independence that the government of France joined with the young American nation to fight against the tyranny symbolized by the British army and its Hessian mercenaries. That belief, however, contains sentimental overtones that do not ring true. That the ideals of "life, liberty and the pursuit of happiness" had a significant influence in determining French foreign policy before 1778, if it is true at all, is true only in small part.—Louis Gottschalk, "The Place of the American Revolution in the Causal Pattern of the French Revolution," 1948

Specific historical evidence to SUPPORT the interpretation above (not mentioned in passage):

_____

_____

_____

_____

_____

Specific historical evidence to SUPPORT the interpretation above (not mentioned in passage):

_____

_____

_____

_____

_____

Specific historical evidence to REFUTE the interpretation above (not mentioned in passage):

_____

_____

_____

_____

_____

Interpretation: Women and France

First, women acquired the nationality of their husbands upon marriage. This made a woman's relationship to the state an indirect one because it was dependent on her husband's. Second, a woman had to reside where her husband desired. Women could not participate in lawsuits or serve as witnesses to civil acts such as births, deaths, and marriages. Such a reduction in woman's civil status enhanced that of the individual male. Moreover, the code reduced, if not eliminated, male accountability for sexual acts and thrust it squarely on women. Women were weakened economically if they bore illegitimate children whereas men were not so affected if they fathered them.—Bonnie G. Smith, "Women and the Napoleonic Code," 1989

It would be wrong to assume that because women had come into the Revolution in 1789 asking for bread and liberty and had come out in 1795 with starvation and restriction of their movements, they had gained nothing. They won laws protecting their rights in marriage, property, and education. True, women were denied political rights in the French Revolution but nowhere else at the time did women share political rights with men.—Ruth Graham, "Loaves and Liberty: Women in the French Revolution," 1977

Specific historical evidence to SUPPORT the interpretation above (not mentioned in passage):

_____

_____

_____

_____

_____

Specific historical evidence to SUPPORT the interpretation above (not mentioned in passage):

_____

_____

_____

_____

Specific historical evidence to REFUTE the interpretation above (not mentioned in passage):

_____

_____

_____

_____

Interpretation: Napoleon

In crowning the work of the Revolution by organizing a government of this type in France, Napoleon obeyed the most powerful political tradition of the age, a mandate more general, more widely endorsed, and more pressing than the demand for social equality or democratic institutions. Read in this light, the significance of his career is seen to lie, not in ten years of revolutionary turmoil from which he sprang, but in the whole century which produced him. . . . The privileged and the unprivileged classes, philosophers, peasants, democrats, and despots all paid homage to this ideal. Napoleon lent his name to an epoch because he symbolized reason enthroned, because he was the philosopher-prince who gave to the dominant aspiration of the age its most typical, most resolute, and most triumphant expression.—Geoffrey Bruun, "Europe and the French Imperium: Napoleon as Enlightened Despot," 1938

Napoleon came to power as a dictatorship from the right–not, of course, as a leader of the old reactionary party, but as a dictator supported by the propertied classes, the financiers and commercial men, the upper bourgeoisie, and speculators, who had made large fortunes out of the revolution and had bought up church or crown lands or the property of émigrés with worthless assignats.—Alfred Cobban, "Dictatorship—Its History and Theory: Napoleon as Dictator," 1939

Specific historical evidence to SUPPORT the interpretation above (not mentioned in passage):

_____

_____

_____

_____

_____

Specific historical evidence to SUPPORT the interpretation above (not mentioned in passage):

_____

_____

_____

_____

_____

Specific historical evidence to REFUTE the interpretation above (not mentioned in passage):

_____

_____

_____

_____

_____

Interpretation: Evaluation of Catherine the Great

Catherine's greatest achievements were in adding territory to the state and in reducing or eliminating the threat to Russian security posed by neighbors to the west and south. . . . The extent of her knowledge and her appetite for reading made her one of the best read women in Europe and the most unusual and outstanding women in Elizabethan Russia. . . . Steeped in Western liberal thought, determined not to dilute her autocratic power but to use it for the benefit of her subjects, Catherine conceived an ambitious plan to provide the nation with a new law code which would reflect Western humanitarian principles. . . . While Catherine did nothing to help landowners' serfs, she certainly improved the lot of state-owned serfs . . . Some new towns came into existence during Catherine's reign. . . . Catherine encouraged foreigners to settle in the thinly populated lands of the empire, allowing them tax exemptions and freedom to practice their religion in the hope that they would set Russians an example of industry and improved farming methods. . . . There was a modest approach to laissez-faire principles in the economic policies of the government under Catherine. . . . Catherine made a beginning on a national system of lay schools.—Melvin C. Wren, *The Course of Russian History*, 1958

No period of Russian history is comparable in outward splendor with the age of Catherine the Great. . . . Yet the brilliant surface of achievement, as so often in Russian history, barely disguised the accumulation of decay. All the glitter of the age was paid for in an aggravation of existing evils. . . . Catherine had no choice but to court the favor of the emancipated nobility. The alliance she struck with them left intact all the prerogatives of autocracy, but for their part it enabled the nobility to stretch authority over their peasants to the point at which they themselves were enthroned as local autocrats. Serfdom was never more inhuman in Russia than in the reign of Catherine the Great.—R. D. Charques, *A Short History of Russia*, 1956

Specific historical evidence to SUPPORT the interpretation above (not mentioned in passage):

_____

_____

_____

_____

_____

Specific historical evidence to SUPPORT the interpretation above (not mentioned in passage):

_____

_____

_____

_____

_____

Specific historical evidence to REFUTE the interpretation above (not mentioned in passage):

_____

_____

_____

_____

_____

Interpretation: Irish Potato Famine

The response of the British government to the Famine was inadequate in terms of humanitarian criteria and, increasingly after 1847, systematically and deliberately so. The localized shortages that followed the blight of 1845 were adequately dealt with but, as the shortages became more widespread, the government retrenched. . . . There was no shortage of resources to avoid the tragedy of a Famine. Within Ireland itself, there were substantial resources of food which, had the political will existed, could have been diverted, even on a short-term measure, to supply a starving people. Instead, the government pursued the objective of economic, social and agrarian reform as a long-term aim, although the price paid for this ultimately delusive goal was privation, disease, emigration, mortality and an enduring legacy of disenchantment.—Christine Kinealy, *This Great Calamity: The Irish Famine 1845–52*, 1995

Sheer numbers also confirm the brutal impact of the Famine. After the four years of continuous blight on the potato crop, the Irish staff of life, at least one million people had vanished. Some were felled by starvation, typhus, and dysentery. In the same year three million were reduced to charity. Others fled the Emerald Isle. The Famine's shadow seems to have left no one untouched. The memory of the starvation and what was considered the inaction of the British (some saw it as pure malice) would, over the course of the next century, become a major weapon of nationalist propaganda. Irish journalists, poets, novelists, and playwrights, would constantly cull the maudlin scenes of those years for pathetic and gripping material. . . . People around the world gasped at the horrors of the Famine. Relief poured in.—Hasia R. Diner, *Erin's Daughters In America: Irish Immigrant Women in the Nineteenth Century*, 1983

Specific historical evidence to SUPPORT the interpretation above (not mentioned in passage):

_____

_____

_____

_____

_____

Specific historical evidence to SUPPORT the interpretation above (not mentioned in passage):

_____

_____

_____

_____

_____

Specific historical evidence to REFUTE the interpretation above (not mentioned in passage):

_____

_____

_____

_____

_____

Interpretation: Romanticism

Another means these poets employed to establish this transcendental order was a vocabulary of assertion, or value-words representing concepts or feelings universally regarded as valuable, such as beauty, truth, liberty; words representative of the highest kind of bond between human beings, such as love, sympathy, harmony; words endowed by religious associations with a special sanctity, such as grace, ministry; or again, words expressive of the greatest human endeavor and aspiration, such as power, might, awful, sublime. . . . This vocabulary provided a context of values for the images, which take on a special character in terms of the value-words, for aspects of the natural world are endowed with the noblest human and religious attributes by their means.—Reginald A. Foakes, *The Romantic Assertion*, 1958

The effects of the Industrial Revolution were not long in appearing. Romanticism prior to 1830 had been mostly negative in nature, concerned primarily with refuting the claims of classical dicta. By 1830 its supporters had made their point by their very victory created for them the problem of establishing a positive creed if they hoped to keep the attention of the public. And it was the Industrial Revolution which . . . furnished the new school with the materials it was seeking, new plots, new characters, new images, even a new purpose for writing, came from this great age of major social change.—Albert Joseph George, *The Development of French Romanticism*, 1955

Specific historical evidence to SUPPORT the interpretation above (not mentioned in passage):

_____

_____

_____

_____

_____

Specific historical evidence to SUPPORT the interpretation above (not mentioned in passage):

_____

_____

_____

_____

_____

Specific historical evidence to REFUTE the interpretation above (not mentioned in passage):

_____

_____

_____

_____

Interpretation: 19th-Century British Imperialism

Much, no doubt, remains to be said concerning the relationship between Empire and economics. But perhaps, when all is said and done, Cecil Rhodes came closest to summing the whole thing up when he said, not totally in jest, that imperialism was nothing more than philanthropy plus 5 percent! But philanthropy for whom? It appears that imperialism can best be viewed as a mechanism for transferring income from the middle to the upper classes. Because of the technology of the imperial machine, the process involved some transfer of those resources to the colonies; however, it is not obvious that either India or the dependent colonies would have chosen to accept that imperial subsidy had they been given the opportunity to object. The Elites and the colonies with responsible government were clear winners; the middle class, certainly, and the dependent Empire, probably, were losers. A strange kind of philanthropy—socialism for the rich, capitalism for the poor.—Lance E. Davis and Robert A. Huttenback, *Mammon and the Pursuit of Empire*, 1988

The Scramble for Africa seems to have emerged from a combination of exaggerated hope and over-heated anxiety. . . . There was, moreover, something irrational about the Partition—as reflected in the grandiose ambitions of [many historical] figures . . . which deeply disturbed the rational minds of politicians . . . In many respects the Scramble was not so much a reaction to events that had already taken place as to events it was feared might take place. It was less the result of a 'general crisis' than a symptom of the anxieties that a general crisis was on the way.—John M. MacKenzie, *The Partition of Africa, 1880–1900*, 1983

Specific historical evidence to SUPPORT the interpretation above (not mentioned in passage):

_____

_____

_____

_____

Specific historical evidence to SUPPORT the interpretation above (not mentioned in passage):

_____

_____

_____

_____

_____

Specific historical evidence to REFUTE the interpretation above (not mentioned in passage):

_____

_____

_____

_____

Interpretation: European Imperialism

Imperialism emerged as the development and direct continuation of fundamental characteristics of capitalism in general. But capitalism only became capitalist imperialism at a definite and very high stage of its development, when certain of its fundamental characteristics began to change into their opposites, when the features of the epoch of transition from capitalism to a higher social and economic system had taken shape and revealed themselves in all spheres. . . . Free competition is the basic feature of capitalism, and of commodity production generally; monopoly is the exact opposite of free competition, but we have seen the latter being transformed into monopoly before our eyes, creating large-scale industry, and carrying concentration of production and capital to the point where out of it has grown and is growing monopoly.—V.I. Lenin, "Imperialism," 1900

The founding of new colonial empires and the fortifying of old ones antedated the establishment of neo-mercantilism, and that the economic arguments adduced in support of imperialism seem to have been a rationalization ex post facto. In the main, it was not Liberal parties, with their super abundance of industrials and bankers, who sponsored the outward imperialistic thrusts of the 1870s and early 1880s. Instead, it was Conservative parties, with a preponderantly agricultural clientele Basically the new imperialism was a nationalistic phenomenon. It followed hard upon the national wars which created an all-powerful Germany and a united Italy, which carried Russia within sight of Constantinople, and which left England fearful and France eclipsed.—Carlton Hayes, "Imperialism as a Nationalistic Phenomenon," 1941

Specific historical evidence to SUPPORT the interpretation above (not mentioned in passage):

_____

_____

_____

_____

_____

Specific historical evidence to SUPPORT the interpretation above (not mentioned in passage):

_____

_____

_____

_____

_____

Specific historical evidence to REFUTE the interpretation above (not mentioned in passage):

_____

_____

_____

_____

Interpretation: Victorian Women

Middle-class women's maternal and housewifely roles were justified in the nineteenth century by a twofold conception of women's nature and capabilities. On the one hand, women were considered passive creatures who were physically and intellectually inferior to men. Thus, women needed protection and direction from their fathers and husbands. On the other hand, women, because they were nonaggressive and sexually passive and were removed from the contamination of the competitive workaday world, were deemed morally superior to men and were to be respected for that. A woman's unique capability and the greatest responsibility in life was caring for the moral and spiritual needs of her family.—Eleanor S. Riemer and John C. Fout, *European Women*, 1980

Unlike more privileged women, working-class women were used to earning income outside the home, and their entry into war work was more likely to be exploitative than liberating. Unlike more privileged women, working-class women and girls had rarely been shielded by a "double standard" of sexual behavior for women and men; rather, working-class women made the maintenance of the double standard possible for men of property. For working-class women in the cities, the growth of the new white-collar jobs was the one trend fostered by the war, which was not reversed afterward. —Bonnie S. Anderson and Judith P. Zinsser, "Women, Work, and World War I," 1999

Specific historical evidence to SUPPORT the interpretation above (not mentioned in passage):

_____

_____

_____

_____

_____

Specific historical evidence to SUPPORT the interpretation above (not mentioned in passage):

_____

_____

_____

_____

_____

Specific historical evidence to REFUTE the interpretation above (not mentioned in passage):

_____

_____

_____

_____

Interpretation: Urbanization

In the last half-century (1848–1898), all the agencies of modern civilization have worked together to abolish this rural isolation; the cities have torn down their fortifications, which separated them from the open country; while the railways, the newspaper press, freedom of migration and settlement, etc., cause the spread of the ideas originating in the cities and lift the people of the rural districts out of their state of mental stagnation. Industry is also carried on outside of the cities, so that the medieval distinction between town and country has lost its meaning in the advanced countries.—Adna Ferrin Weber, *The Growth of Cities in the Nineteenth Century*, 1963

If farmers live in the city while artisans and traders are absent from the countryside, then levels of urbanization will be higher than in intermediate situations. There are also differences in the density of the occupation of agricultural land, differences largely determined not only by the quality of the land, the climate and the level of technology, but also by the dominant type of food crop: rice, maize, and potatoes, for example, permit more people per hectare than wheat. It is at this point, moreover, that the tyranny of distance intervenes. For it remains necessary to transport the agricultural surplus to the city; and beyond a certain distance, varying as a function of geographic and technological conditions, the surplus ceases to have any value.—Paul Bairoch, *Cities and Economic Development*, 1988

Specific historical evidence to SUPPORT the interpretation above (not mentioned in passage):

_____

_____

_____

_____

_____

Specific historical evidence to SUPPORT the interpretation above (not mentioned in passage):

_____

_____

_____

_____

_____

Specific historical evidence to REFUTE the interpretation above (not mentioned in passage):

_____

_____

_____

_____

_____

Interpretation: Causes of World War I

Foreign-policy issues became highly politicized, since notwithstanding governmental appeals, the primacy of foreign policy is inoperative under prerevolutionary conditions. Whereas the campaign against the arms race was an integral part of the struggle against the forces of order, the campaign for preparedness was a central feature of the struggle against the forces of change. . . . To a not inconsiderable degree, then, throughout Europe the rising international tensions were accompanied by rising internal tensions—by mounting social, political, and economic struggles that radicalized the extremes, eroded the center, and inclined the governments to push preparedness and diplomatic obduracy as part of their efforts to maintain a precarious domestic status quo.—Arno J. Mayer, "Domestic Causes of the First World War," 1967

In the last analysis, we may conclude, the causes of the First World War must be sought not in the blunders and miscalculations of the governments alone, but in the fact that Germany's governmental system, as well as Austria-Hungary's and Russia's, was no longer adequate in the face of rapid social change and the steady advance of mass politics.—Wolfgang J. Mommsen, *Domestic Factors in German Foreign Policy Before 1914*, 1973

Specific historical evidence to SUPPORT the interpretation above (not mentioned in passage):

_____

_____

_____

_____

_____

Specific historical evidence to SUPPORT the interpretation above (not mentioned in passage):

_____

_____

_____

_____

Specific historical evidence to REFUTE the interpretation above (not mentioned in passage):

_____

_____

_____

_____

_____

Interpretation: World War I

Allies had won the war between July and November 1918. The German army was defeated on the Western Front; that the British army played a leading role in that victory; that the contribution of the Americans, except in terms of morale, was minor; and that the British generals were not 'donkeys' but men who did their best with the technology they had in appalling conditions. Further, there had been no easy way to win the war in the trenches. Since the French insisted that their territory be liberated, tanks and planes were as yet primitive and Germany had no 'soft underbelly,' it was necessary to defeat the main strength of the German army on the Western Front and that inevitably involved very costly offensives.—John Terraine, *To Win A War: 1918, the Year of Victory*, 2008

The war was not inevitable. The British were not obliged to declare war on Germany when they did; and that the Germans very nearly won the war in 1914 and would almost certainly have done so if the British had not intervened. These are not particularly controversial statements, but Ferguson also postulates that the result of a German victory would have been 'something like the European Union', half a century ahead of its time: a German-led association of states in Europe, much like we have now, but without the catastrophic damage inflicted on all sides by the events of 1915–18.—Niall Ferguson, "The Kaiser's European Union," 2000

Specific historical evidence to SUPPORT the interpretation above (not mentioned in passage):

_____

_____

_____

_____

_____

Specific historical evidence to SUPPORT the interpretation above (not mentioned in passage):

_____

_____

_____

_____

Specific historical evidence to REFUTE the interpretation above (not mentioned in passage):

_____

_____

_____

_____

_____

Interpretation: Russian Revolution

Anti-Communist interpretations, however they may deplore the October Revolution, are almost as heavily inclined to view it as the inescapable outcome of overwhelming circumstances or of long and diabolical planning. The impasse of the war was to blame, or Russia's inexperience in democracy, or the feverish laws of revolution. If not these factors, it was Lenin's genius and trickery in propaganda, or the party organization as his trusty and invincible instrument. Of course, all of these considerations played a part, but when they were weighed against the day-by-day record of the revolution, it is hard to argue that any combination of them made Bolshevik power inevitable or even likely.—Robert V. Daniels, *Red October: The Bolshevik Revolution of 1917*, 1967

An unsuccessful war is never popular, and the war of 1914–1917 on the Russian front was unsuccessful. Russian causalities were officially estimated at over 7 million, half of them missing and prisoners-of-war. According to confidential official records, refusals to fight and mass surrender to the enemy began in 1914 and became widespread during the retreat in 1915. The Russian steamroller, in which the Western allies put their hope in the dark hours of the war, did not come up to expectation. Food shortages, the patent inability of the government to cope with mounting emergencies, frustration, and near chaos bred weariness, disaffection, and disillusionment. It is the sum total of these conditions that spelled the end of the monarchy and made the revolution inevitable.—Michael T. Florinsky, "The February Revolution in Russia," 1969

Specific historical evidence to SUPPORT the interpretation above (not mentioned in passage):

_____

_____

_____

_____

_____

Specific historical evidence to SUPPORT the interpretation above (not mentioned in passage):

_____

_____

_____

_____

_____

Specific historical evidence to REFUTE the interpretation above (not mentioned in passage):

_____

_____

_____

_____

_____

Interpretation: Hitler and World War II

Hitler's foreign policy was, therefore, in no way independent of 'structural determinants' of different kinds. These, however, pushed him if anything still faster on the path he was in any case determined to tread. When all due consideration is given to the actions—and grave mistakes—of other governments in the diplomatic turmoil of the 1930s, the crucial and pivotal role of Germany as the active catalyst in the upheaval is undeniable. Many of the developments which took place were in certain respect likely if not inevitable as the unfinished business of the First World War and the post-war settlement. The continuities in German foreign policy after 1933 are manifest, and formed part of the basis of the far-reaching identity of interest—certainly until 1937–8—of the conservative elites with the Nazi leadership, rooted in the pursuit of a traditional German power policy aimed at attaining hegemony in central Europe. At the same time, important strands of discontinuity and an unquestionable new dynamism were also unmistakable hallmarks of German foreign policy after 1933—such that one can speak with justification of a 'diplomatic revolution' in Europe by 1936.—Ian Kershaw, *The Nazi Dictatorship: Problems and Perspectives of Interpretation*, 1993

Specific historical evidence to SUPPORT the interpretation above (not mentioned in passage):

_____

_____

_____

_____

_____

Specific historical evidence to SUPPORT the interpretation above (not mentioned in passage):

_____

_____

_____

_____

_____

Specific historical evidence to REFUTE the interpretation above (not mentioned in passage):

_____

_____

_____

_____

_____

Interpretation: World War II and the Bomb

President Truman used the [atomic] bomb more to impress the Russians and improve his bargaining position with them than to subdue the Japanese. Secretary of State James Byrnes, for example, told the American ambassador to the Soviet Union, Joseph E. Davies, that "American possession of the bomb would have some effect on the Soviets and induce them to yield and agree to our position."—Gar Alperovitz, *Atomic Diplomacy*, 1965

Justifying the costs of the Manhattan Project was [a reason]. How could the government spend $2 billion, and employ the efforts of 600,000 workers, and then not employ and demonstrate the results.—J. Samuel Walker, *Prompt and Utter Destruction*, 1997

Specific historical evidence to SUPPORT the interpretation above (not mentioned in passage):

_____
_____
_____
_____
_____

Specific historical evidence to SUPPORT the interpretation above (not mentioned in passage):

_____
_____
_____
_____
_____

Specific historical evidence to REFUTE the interpretation above (not mentioned in passage):

_____
_____
_____
_____
_____

Interpretation: Cold War

The Cold War had now begun. It was the product not of a decision but of a dilemma. Each side felt compelled to adopt policies which the other could not but regard as a threat to the principles of the peace. Each then felt compelled to undertake defensive measures. Thus the Russians saw no choice but to consolidate their security in Eastern Europe. The Americans, regarding Eastern Europe as the first step toward Western Europe, responded by asserting their interest in the zone the Russians deemed vital to their security. The Russians concluded that the West was resuming its old course of capitalist encirclement; that it was purposefully laying the foundation for anti-Soviet regimes in the area defined by the blood of centuries as crucial to Russian survival.—Arthur Schlesinger, Jr., *Origins of the Cold War*, 1967

In grim battles against their enemies, the Soviet people victoriously defended their Socialist achievements, the most progressive social and political system, and the freedom and independence of the U.S.S.R., and strengthened the security of their state frontiers. [. . .] By their heroic war effort the Soviet people saved the peoples of Europe from the yoke of German imperialism. The Red Army, assisted by the peoples of Europe, expelled the German fascist invaders from Poland, Czechoslovakia, Yugoslavia, Bulgaria, Rumania, Hungary, Austria, Denmark and northern Norway, fulfilling with honor its liberating mission. . . . The main foreign policy aim of the Party was to secure a stable and lasting peace, to strengthen Socialism's position in the world arena.—B.N. Ponomaryov, "The Cold War: The Communist Perspective," 1960

Specific historical evidence to SUPPORT the interpretation above (not mentioned in passage):

_____

_____

_____

_____

_____

Specific historical evidence to SUPPORT the interpretation above (not mentioned in passage):

_____

_____

_____

_____

_____

Specific historical evidence to REFUTE the interpretation above (not mentioned in passage):

_____

_____

_____

_____

_____

Interpretation: International Security

First, the great powers of Western Europe, France and West Germany most notably, have ceased preparing for war against one another. We now tend to take the new West European security community for granted. But our nonchalance must not blur the fact that the emergencies of a 'no war' community on the Continent between 1945 and 1955 was a historically momentous occurrence. . . . Second, aspects of the national sovereignty and governmental prerogative of several Western European states have been voluntarily transferred to regional policy-making bodies. Over several years these international organizations and supranational institutions have grown in stature in the estimations of European elites.—Donald J. Puchala, "Patterns in West European Integration," 2008

With its constitution, it is extremely difficult for the United Nations to exercise an influence on problems which are clearly and definitely within the orbit of present-day conflicts between power blocs. . . . This clearly defines the main field of useful activity of the United Nations in its efforts to prevent conflicts or to solve conflicts. . . . The United Nations should seek to bring such conflicts out of this sphere through solutions aiming, in the first instance, at their strict localization. In doing so, the Organization and its agents have to lay down a policy line, but this will then not be for one party against another, but for the general purpose of avoiding an extension or achieving a reduction of the area into which the bloc conflicts penetrate.—Dag Hammarskjold, "The Positive Role of the United Nations in a Split World," 1960

Specific historical evidence to SUPPORT the interpretation above (not mentioned in passage):

_____

_____

_____

_____

_____

Specific historical evidence to SUPPORT the interpretation above (not mentioned in passage):

_____

_____

_____

_____

_____

Specific historical evidence to REFUTE the interpretation above (not mentioned in passage):

_____

_____

_____

_____

_____

Interpretation: Decline of Western Civilization

The disintegration of the Soviet Union removed the only serious challenger to the West and as a result the world is and will be shaped by the goals, priorities, and interests of the principal Western nations, with perhaps an occasional assist from Japan. As the one remaining superpower, the United States together with Britain and France make the crucial decisions on political and security issues; the United States together with Germany and Japan make the crucial decisions on economic issues. The West is the only civilization which has substantial interests in every other civilization or region and has the ability to affect the politics, economics, and security of every other civilization or region. Societies from other civilizations usually need Western help to achieve their goals and protect their interests.
—Samuel P. Huntington, *The Clash of Civilizations and the Remaking of World Order*, 1996

The second picture of the West is very different. It is of a civilization in decline, its share of world political, economic, and military power going down relative to that of other civilizations. The West's victory in the Cold War has produced not triumph but exhaustion. The West is increasingly concerned with its internal problems and needs, as it confronts slow economic growth, stagnating populations, unemployment, huge government deficits, a declining work ethic, low savings rates, and in many countries including the United States social disintegration, drugs, and crime. Economic power is rapidly shifting to East Asia, and military power and political influence are starting to follow. India is on the verge of economic takeoff and the Islamic world is increasingly hostile toward the West. The willingness of other societies to accept the West's dictates or abide its sermons is rapidly evaporating, and so are the West's self-confidence and will to dominate. The late 1980s witnessed much debate about the declinist thesis concerning the United States.—Samuel P. Huntington, *The Clash of Civilizations and the Remaking of World Order*, 1996

Specific historical evidence to SUPPORT the interpretation above (not mentioned in passage):

_____

_____

_____

_____

_____

Specific historical evidence to SUPPORT the interpretation above (not mentioned in passage):

_____

_____

_____

_____

_____

Specific historical evidence to REFUTE the interpretation above (not mentioned in passage):

_____

_____

_____

_____

_____

Student Instructions: Chronological Reasoning

When we are asked to use chronological reasoning, we place a variety of events into historical order. Although it might not seem important to know historical dates, the reality is that dates help us to conceptualize important trends. Understanding when and why things occurred is critical to understanding history. It would be impossible to practice many, if not all, of this workbook's historical thinking skills without the proper chronology of content.

The purpose of the Chronological Reasoning activities is not only to practice placing a number of historical events in the correct order but also to understand how and why things occurred based on that order. This practice will help reinforce your knowledge of the given historical period and will encourage you to think about how these events relate to each other.

Chronological Reasoning: Renaissance (Example)

Spain Unified under Isabella and Ferdinand	Columbus Sails for Americas
Medici Establish Influence in Florence	Fall of Florentine Republic
Printing Press Invented	Ottoman Conquest of Constantinople
War of the Roses	Treaty of Lodi
Inquisition Carried Out in Spain	
End of English Civil Wars	

1ST EVENT   Medici Establish Influence in Florence

2ND EVENT   Printing Press Invented

3RD EVENT   Ottoman Conquest of Constantinople

4TH EVENT   Treaty of Lodi

5TH EVENT   War of the Roses

6TH EVENT   Inquisition Carried Out in Spain

7TH EVENT   Spain Unified under Isabella and Ferdinand

8TH EVENT   Columbus Sails for Americas

9TH EVENT   Fall of Florentine Republic

10TH EVENT   End of English Civil Wars

CR1

Chronological Reasoning: Renaissance

Spain Unified under Isabella and Ferdinand	Columbus Sails for Americas
Medici Establish Influence in Florence	Fall of Florentine Republic
Printing Press Invented	Ottoman Conquest of Constantinople
War of the Roses	Treaty of Lodi
Inquisition Carried Out in Spain	
End of English Civil Wars	

1ST EVENT _____

2ND EVENT _____

3RD EVENT _____

4TH EVENT _____

5TH EVENT _____

6TH EVENT _____

7TH EVENT _____

8TH EVENT _____

9TH EVENT _____

10TH EVENT _____

Chronological Reasoning: Reformation

More Writes *Utopia*	Peace of Augsburg
Treaty of Cateau-Cambresis	Jesuits Established as New Catholic
German Peasants' War	Order
Catholic Council of Trent	Act of Supremacy
Calvin Publishes *Institutes*	
Luther Composes 95 Theses	
Charles V's Sack of Rome	

1ST EVENT   _____

2ND EVENT   _____

3RD EVENT   _____

4TH EVENT   _____

5TH EVENT   _____

6TH EVENT   _____

7TH EVENT   _____

8TH EVENT   _____

9TH EVENT   _____

10TH EVENT   _____

Chronological Reasoning: Century of Crisis

French Wars of Religion Begin

Peace of Westphalia

Battle of Lepanto

French Join Thirty Years' War

St. Bartholomew's Day Massacre

Defeat of Spanish Armada

Galileo Recants Support of
    Heliocentrism

English Puritans Set Up Massachusetts
    Bay Company

Edict of Nantes

Beginning of Thirty Years' War

1ST EVENT _____

2ND EVENT _____

3RD EVENT _____

4TH EVENT _____

5TH EVENT _____

6TH EVENT _____

7TH EVENT _____

8TH EVENT _____

9TH EVENT _____

10TH EVENT _____

Chronological Reasoning: State Building and Search for Order

Beginning of English Civil War between Charles I and Parliament

Execution of Charles I

Monarchy Restored in England

William and Mary

Newton Publishes *Principia Mathematica*

Louis XIV Revokes Edict of Nantes

Austrian Habsburgs Break Turkish Siege of Vienna

Hobbes Publishes *Leviathan*

Locke Publishes *Two Treatises of Government*

Molière Publishes *The Middle-Class Gentleman*

1ST EVENT _____

2ND EVENT _____

3RD EVENT _____

4TH EVENT _____

5TH EVENT _____

6TH EVENT _____

7TH EVENT _____

8TH EVENT _____

9TH EVENT _____

10TH EVENT _____

CR5

Chronological Reasoning: Atlantic System

Bank of England Established

Handel Composes *Messiah*

Bayle Publishes *Historical and Critical Dictionary*

War of Polish Succession

Turks Recognize Habsburg Rule

Peace of Utrecht

Death of Louis XIV

Last Outbreak of Bubonic Plague

Peter the Great Begins Construction of St. Petersburg

Treaty of Nystad

1ST EVENT _____

2ND EVENT _____

3RD EVENT _____

4TH EVENT _____

5TH EVENT _____

6TH EVENT _____

7TH EVENT _____

8TH EVENT _____

9TH EVENT _____

10TH EVENT _____

Chronological Reasoning: Enlightenment

Ratification of the U.S. Constitution	Seven Years' War
War of Austrian Succession	American Declaration of Independence
Encyclopedia Published in France	Catherine the Great's Charter of the
Kant Publishes *Critique of Pure Reason*	Nobility
Joseph II Reform Program Begins	
Pugachev Rebellion of Russian Peasants	
First Partition of Poland	

1ST EVENT _____

_____

2ND EVENT _____

_____

3RD EVENT _____

_____

4TH EVENT _____

_____

5TH EVENT _____

_____

6TH EVENT _____

_____

7TH EVENT _____

_____

8TH EVENT _____

_____

9TH EVENT _____

_____

10TH EVENT _____

Chronological Reasoning: French Revolution

Beginning of French Revolution

Napoleon Comes to Power

Abolition of Slavery in French Colonies

Beginning of Slave Revolt in
Saint-Domingue

Dutch Patriot Revolt Stifled by Prussian
Invasion

Second Partition of Poland

Collapse of Resistance in Austrian
Netherlands

Second Revolution and the Overthrow of
the French Monarchy

Third Partition of Poland

Robespierre's Government by Terror Falls

1ST EVENT _____

2ND EVENT _____

3RD EVENT _____

4TH EVENT _____

5TH EVENT _____

6TH EVENT _____

7TH EVENT _____

8TH EVENT _____

9TH EVENT _____

10TH EVENT _____

Chronological Reasoning: Napoleon and the Revolutionary Legacy

Napoleon Named First Consul

English Parliament Passes Reform Bill

Napoleon Invades Russia

Congress of Vienna

Beethoven Publishes *Ninth Symphony*

Shelly Publishes *Frankenstein*

Decembrist Revolt

Manchester and Liverpool Railway
   Opens in England

Napoleon Signs a Concordat with Pope

Napoleon Defeated at Waterloo

1ST EVENT _____

_____

2ND EVENT _____

_____

3RD EVENT _____

_____

4TH EVENT _____

_____

5TH EVENT _____

_____

6TH EVENT _____

_____

7TH EVENT _____

_____

8TH EVENT _____

_____

9TH EVENT _____

_____

10TH EVENT _____

Chronological Reasoning: Industrialization and Urbanization

Cholera Epidemic Sweeps Across Europe
Crystal Palace Exhibition in London
France Begins Conquest of Algeria
Bronte Publishes *Jane Eyre*
German Zollverein Established Under
   Prussian Leadership

British and Foreign Temperance Society
   Established
Beginning of Opium War
Famine Strikes Ireland
Marx and Engels Publish *Communist
   Manifesto*
Factory Act

1ST EVENT ————————————————————————

2ND EVENT ————————————————————————

3RD EVENT ————————————————————————

4TH EVENT ————————————————————————

5TH EVENT ————————————————————————

6TH EVENT ————————————————————————

7TH EVENT ————————————————————————

8TH EVENT ————————————————————————

9TH EVENT ————————————————————————

10TH EVENT ————————————————————————

Chronological Reasoning: Politics and Culture of the Nation-State

Franco-Prussian War
Start of Crimean War
British Suppression of Indian Rebellion
U.S. Civil War
Meiji Restoration Begins in Japan
Second Reform Bill in England
German Empire Proclaimed at Versailles

Women's College Founded at Cambridge
  University
Abolition of Serfdom in Russia

1ST EVENT _____

_____

2ND EVENT _____

_____

3RD EVENT _____

_____

4TH EVENT _____

_____

5TH EVENT _____

_____

6TH EVENT _____

_____

7TH EVENT _____

_____

8TH EVENT _____

_____

9TH EVENT _____

_____

10TH EVENT _____

Chronological Reasoning: Industry, Empire, and Everyday Life

British Parliament Passes Reform Act

Extended Economic Recession Begins

Beginning of Bismarck's Social Welfare
    Legislation

Establishment of the Second International

Triple Alliance Formed

Dual Alliance Formed

Invention of the Telephone

Beginning of the Berlin Conference

Beginning of Impressionism

Beginning of New Imperialism

1ST EVENT   _____

2ND EVENT   _____

3RD EVENT   _____

4TH EVENT   _____

5TH EVENT   _____

6TH EVENT   _____

7TH EVENT   _____

8TH EVENT   _____

9TH EVENT   _____

10TH EVENT   _____

Chronological Reasoning: Modernity and the Road to War

Dreyfus Affair

Assassination of Austrian Archduke
Ferdinand

Japan Defeats Russia in Russo-Japanese War

Start of Boer War

Freud Publishes *The Interpretation of
Dreams*

Establishment of the Women's Social
and Political Union

Women Receive Vote in Finland

Young Turks Revolt

China Declared a Republic

Einstein Publishes *Special Theory of
Relativity*

1ST EVENT _____

2ND EVENT _____

3RD EVENT _____

4TH EVENT _____

5TH EVENT _____

6TH EVENT _____

7TH EVENT _____

8TH EVENT _____

9TH EVENT _____

10TH EVENT _____

Chronological Reasoning: World War I and Reconstruction

WWI Begins

Crash of Stock Market in U.S.

Lenin Dies

Easter Uprising Against British Rule

Bolshevik Revolution

Establishment of Weimar Republic

Paris Peace Conference Redraws Map of
  Europe

Eliot Publishes *The Waste Land*

Overturn of Tsarist Autocracy

U.S. Enters WWI

1ST EVENT   _____

            _____

2ND EVENT   _____

            _____

3RD EVENT   _____

            _____

4TH EVENT   _____

            _____

5TH EVENT   _____

            _____

6TH EVENT   _____

            _____

7TH EVENT   _____

            _____

8TH EVENT   _____

            _____

9TH EVENT   _____

            _____

10TH EVENT _____

Chronological Reasoning: Age of Catastrophes

Global Depression Begins	Battle of Britain
Fall of Berlin	Japan Attacks Pearl Harbor
Allied Forces Land at Normandy	WWII Ends
France Falls to German Army	Beginning of Spanish Civil War
Woolf Publishes *Three Guineas*	
Show Trials Begin in USSR	
Hitler Comes to Power in Germany	

1ST EVENT _____

2ND EVENT _____

3RD EVENT _____

4TH EVENT _____

5TH EVENT _____

6TH EVENT _____

7TH EVENT _____

8TH EVENT _____

9TH EVENT _____

10TH EVENT _____

Chronological Reasoning: Cold War in Europe

Cuban Missile Crisis	USSR Launches Sputnik
Nationalization of the Suez Canal	Mao Zedong Leads Communist
Israel Established	Revolution in China
Stalin Dies	End of Korean War
Vietnamese Forces Defeat French	Independence of India and Pakistan from
Simone de Beauvior Publishes *The*	Britain
Second Sex	

1ST EVENT _____

2ND EVENT _____

3RD EVENT _____

4TH EVENT _____

5TH EVENT _____

6TH EVENT _____

7TH EVENT _____

8TH EVENT _____

9TH EVENT _____

10TH EVENT _____

Chronological Reasoning: Postindustrial Society and the End of the Cold War

Vatican II Reforms

Chinese Student Revolt in Tiananmen
  Square

Revolution of Czechoslovakia

U.S. Astronauts Walk on Moon

International Year of Women

SALT I Treaty

End of Vietnam War

OPEC Oil Embargo on West

Reagan Becomes U.S. President

Gorbachev Comes to Power in USSR

1ST EVENT _____

_____

2ND EVENT _____

_____

3RD EVENT _____

_____

4TH EVENT _____

_____

5TH EVENT _____

_____

6TH EVENT _____

_____

7TH EVENT _____

_____

8TH EVENT _____

_____

9TH EVENT _____

_____

10TH EVENT _____

CR-17